somewhere under the rainbow

somewhere under the rainbow

My Walk With God Through Depression, Bipolar Disorder, VNS Therapy

marla k. chudy

Tate Publishing & *Enterprises*

Published by Tate Publishing & Enterprises, LLC
127 E. Trade Center Terrace | Mustang, Oklahoma 73064 USA
1.888.361.9473 | www.tatepublishing.com

Tate Publishing is committed to excellence in the publishing industry. The company reflects the philosophy established by the founders, based on Psalm 68:11,
"The Lord gave the word and great was the company of those who published it."

Cover design by Isaiah R. McKee
Interior design by Nathan Harmony

Published in the United States of America

ISBN: 978-1-60462-903-3
1. Christian Living: Practical Living: Grief, Suffering, Consolation
2. Motivational: Biography & Autobiography
08.03.18

Dedication

Dedicated to my mother, father, and brother who cared for me and loved me through both the good times and bad. And to my son, Steven, who will always be my cheerleader and my inspiration. Also to my ex-husband, Ted, who raised our son, during my physical and mental absence, to be the wonderful man that he is today.

It is to all of you that I express my deepest gratitude. God Bless You!

I thank God for his beloved Son, Jesus Christ, who died on the cross, shedding his blood for my sins. I thank him also for the wisdom, energy, and perseverance to write this book. Thank you, Jesus!

Acknowledgments

I want to thank Dr. Gregory Kasper of Toledo, Ohio, and St. Vincent Mercy Medical Center for their kindness and generosity. I send a special thank you to the VNS Therapy Access Program, which made my surgery possible. Thanks to Bridget Tubriby, my Nurse Case Manager at Cyberonics ©, who was always there to walk me through the obstacles, always helpful and pleasant and who showed sincere empathy for my situation. In addition, I want to express a special thank you to my psychiatrist, Dr. Cynthia Evans of Fremont, Ohio, for her patience, support, and willingness to learn about VNS Therapy. Thank you for not giving up on me.

I send a special thank you to all my relatives, friends, and church members who prayed for me and were always there to support me.

I would like to thank all my readers for taking the time to read my story. If I can help just one person understand depression and bipolar disorder better, or if my book can help keep just one person from committing suicide, then I am grateful and this book has served its purpose.

It is to all of you that I express my deepest gratitude. God Bless You!

Contents

Introduction

It is said that we learn by our experiences in life. We take these experiences with us into our future. My mind, from my early childhood, however, is strewed about irregularly. There are many events that I've been told about, but cannot account for. Whatever the time period, whatever the situation, I missed out on what others thought were significant circumstances. My brain seems to remember only innocuous accumulations of events insignificant to others, but monumental to me. I didn't start remembering bits and pieces of my life until I was five years old and then it was only in spurts of recollection, devoid of personality.

I've asked myself many times what I want this book to be about. What do I want to tell people about the cold unrelenting darkness of depression and the hushed secrets that were never to be revealed? Depression surrounded me as if I was in a time capsule buried in the ground—small, dark, cold, and damp. I thought there was no way out. I was in the clutches of a demon that wanted to devour me. Depression made me feel as if no one cared. I was lonely, I ached, I sobbed uncontrollably, and I would curl up into a little ball in my closet in excruciating mental and physical pain. I lived in my bedroom when I was young. It was my safe place.

I would struggle to get a whiff of fresh air as I sat in my quiet, 10' by 10' bedroom behind a closed door. The bedroom had a twin bed, a set of dresser drawers, and two tiny windows draped with tiered curtains. However, it was the six foot, split closet that I was obsessed with. It had shelves on the left side and hanging clothes on the right. It was a hiding place for my mind. I could crawl into it and no one could see me. I was safe. I had a recurring daydream that I was floating up above the shelves in this closet. Floating like a colorful helium balloon, just hovering, gazing around the room as if weightless. I felt so carefree and alive. It was like being in space where if I moved my arms and legs my body would turn and float in air. I would fly out of the closet and drift slowly away. Suddenly, I would feel as if an invisible driving force was beckoning me back into my safety zone, and my legs and arms would start to thrash wildly to get back. The entire event was inexplicable by ordinary means, yet it was very real to me.

Those childhood memories that I do recall are as vivid

as bright red roses. Ah yes, the reminiscences of static spaces in time, experiences that I would not realize would impact my life thirty-five to forty years down the road. The need to achieve perfection comes to mind in a recurring nightmare I had as a young teenager.

I was at my maternal grandparents' house. They had a two-story home situated several feet from a dirt road with a quaint little front porch from which one could see Lake Erie. From the front porch one walked into a living room/dining room area. The living room had a couch, four chairs, a television set, and a couple of end tables, along with a number of antique floor lamps. The dining room had a huge wooden desk with a large beveled glass mirror hanging over it and a foldaway dining room table that was only opened on special occasions. All the rooms had old-fashioned radiators with hot water heat surging through the pipes to take the chill out of the wintry air. Just off the dining room were the kitchen and a large bathroom/laundry room combination. There was also a harrowing door off this room that led to a cold, clammy, ghost-filled basement. One could access the upstairs from the dining room area. There was a set of stairs with a landing and then another set of stairs that led to four upstairs bedrooms and a tiny bath. My grandmother had hung a heavy wool curtain between the landing and the first set of stairs that led to the dining room in order to keep the downstairs warm and the bedrooms cool.

As a young teenager I kept having this recurring nightmare, too many times to count, that I was standing on the landing and desperately clinging to that curtain for my life. I imagined that a man with strong muscular arms and a tall stature was pushing me, fighting with me, and frantically trying to hurl me down the carpeted stairs. I could smell his body odor as if he had been working in the hot summer sun for hours and pictured him as unshaven and disheveled, even though I never saw him. Every nightmare had the same ending. The curtain tore as I struggled to maintain my footing and I fell in slow motion down the stairs, only stopping when my head hit the radiator below. Many years later as I recounted the nightmare, a friend told me that I was the one pushing myself down the stairs. When I hit the radiator below and awoke from my nightmare it was a good sign. It meant that I would wake up and realize that I was pushing myself too hard to be a perfectionist–to get straight A's in school, to dress properly in dark blue suits and stark black heeled shoes, to have my hair meticulously groomed and my nails manicured. I had to smile all the time to cover up the pain, greet everyone politely, speak proper English, and observe proper etiquette. I expected myself to be prim, proper, and modest in every circumstance. Marla had to be perfect! I realized later in life that this was impossible to achieve.

This book, however, is not about nightmares or imaginary floating. It is not about a fictional character who is trying to "find herself." It is about truth, reality, and factual feelings that have built up inside of me for more than fifty years, feelings that came from a brain hungering for the chemicals it so badly needed. Can it all be blamed on a chemical imbalance? Maybe it could, maybe not. I made some bad decisions and poor judgments, but how responsible was the chemical imbalance for those bad decisions and poor judgments? My psychiatrists have told me the chemical imbalance was to blame, but who can assess blame to the unknown?

Close relationships with caring, loving friends were severed because of my deep depressions and wild, critical outbursts. It is difficult to be around someone who is habitually depressed and then suddenly becomes angry and spiteful in the blink of an eye. Jobs came and went as I became disenchanted with my first job, anxiety ridden with my second, and started losing my temper as I progressed to higher levels of responsibility. Life was unpredictable at every turn and I could go from normal to psychotic within minutes.

Nevertheless, I would learn and grow, swallow the right medications, and swallow the wrong. Most medications did not work beyond a brief time. The plunges into that deep dark hole in the ground where I thrashed about desperately trying to reach the last rung of the ladder as the dirt walls were crumbling around me, the small light shining at the end of a tunnel and the horrendous ups and downs are real. I wasn't on medications, or I was on the wrong medications when that deep dark hole appeared. I didn't know at the time what was right and what was wrong, I was simply following my doctor's orders like a puppet. If I can help just one person who has not experienced the disease to understand depression and bipolar disorder, or give hope to someone who is in the midst of it, I've done what I set out to do. This is my story.

Reflections of My Childhood

"Very early in the morning, while it was still dark, Jesus got up, left the house and went off to a solitary place, where he prayed," (Mark 1:35, NIV).

Looking out the large picture window from the tiny living room of our eight hundred square foot home, I could almost smell the fresh cut green grass. A premature blue spruce tree stood under my bedroom window and a tall sturdy maple tree graced the U-shaped driveway on the left side of the house. As I continued to gaze out the window, I wondered where my life would take me. As a child, I assumed I would live in this same small house forever. I realized, in my teens, that my childhood was a void, a vast windswept desert with no color, no footsteps, and no destination.

I grew up in a small town in northern Ohio called Lakeside. It was a beautiful little town situated on Lake Erie and consisted mostly of summer cottages. The year-round residents were the kind of folks who knew everyone and everything that was happening. There were only two stop signs in the small downtown and only the main roads were paved. The streets were mostly dirt roads and green grass was sparse. I remember hearing the message that Christ died on the cross for my sins, but as a child I never fully understood or appreciated that fact. Oh, I believed it because the Bible said so, but I never understood the tremendous impact it would have on my life as I grew up.

It was a unique town in that there were around one hundred to one hundred and fifty people who lived there year-round. However, for two weeks in June of each year the town swelled with 2,500 preachers attending the Annual East and West Ohio Methodist Conferences. Ministers came from all across Ohio to create legislation for the Methodist church. They would sing, worship, and praise God for all the wonderful things he was doing.

My maternal grandparents operated a small family grocery store in the middle of town. Mounted on top of the structure was a huge siren that blared out its tone to summon firefighters in case of an emergency. The town had no radios or scanners, just the high-pitched siren. The inside of the store consisted of oiled wooden floors, a counter for fruits and vegetables, and a meat market where nothing was ever pre-packaged, but always weighed out to the customer's specifications.

Some of my best memories were working in the store. I helped mark the price on cans of soup with a large black magic marker (thirteen cents for a can of Campbell's tomato soup) and I helped stock shelves with everything from pickles to toilet paper.

The store had a coal furnace with only one large vent into the building and no air conditioning. We would stop at the store after school on a wintry day and I would immediately run back to the vent to swallow up the heat. My dress would billow up like a big puff of smoke. I guess I wasn't very modest at that age.

When we were older, the summer group, which consisted mostly of PKs (preachers' kids) and the hometown kids, spent hours playing games and having picnics together. It was great fun, and I was care-free.

Winter was a stark contrast to the summer, when so many visitors occupied the town. The small community dwindled down to just the locals, and the winter activities began. Sled riding and ice skating were popular. I remember a day when ice and snow had fallen on the roads overnight. I was sliding on ice in front of our home with my brother and his friend Larry. It must have been fun, I just don't recall. I fell and hit my head so hard that I lapsed into unconsciousness. I'm told my brother carried me back to the house with my left arm draped over his strong shoulder and my right arm swinging freely. His friend, and I use the term loosely, seemed to think it was funny and ran up behind me, grabbing my right arm and watching it fall lifelessly back to my body. I remember lying on the couch in our small living room, vomiting into the infamous, scratched, silver-coated vomit pan. I only recall bits and pieces of the afternoon because I kept drifting in and out of consciousness. I wondered why no one seemed to be very concerned about me at the time. I couldn't understand why no one seemed to care. I came in the house unconscious and yet no one called an ambulance or took me to the doctor or hospital. I was scared! Nothing like this had ever happened to me before.

I grew up in a family that didn't show outward signs of affection. The love was there, it was just hidden. My mother was beautiful, thoughtful, and kind. My father worked hard to support the family and loved us very much. They were wonderful parents who would have done anything for my brother and me.

My childhood seemed normal. I wasn't showing signs of depression. I was having fun with the neighborhood kids. I grew up like most kids did in that day and age. I got into trouble occasionally and was appropriately disciplined. My brother and I had many predictable disagreements and went through the typical sibling rivalry stage. Being the boy in the family, he could always get away with more than I ever could! Nevertheless, he always stuck up for me if someone else was causing me trouble.

The best time we had was when our family took a car

trip to visit my dad's relatives in Arizona. The car was not air-conditioned and the temperatures were in the nineties and hundreds, but that didn't matter. We had the time of our lives swimming in my uncle's kidney-shaped swimming pool, admiring the beautiful palm trees, which we had never seen before, eating oranges and grapefruit straight off the tree, and visiting Carlsbad Caverns, in New Mexico, on the way home. It was the best time of my childhood and I know my parents did it on a shoestring budget.

On another trip my mother, brother, and I flew to Texas to see my mother's relatives. Unfortunately, my dad had to stay home and work, but the rest of us went on our merry way. This was my first airplane ride and I was so excited. I loved it! Everything from the roar of the engines and being thrust back in my seat as the airplane was taking off, to coming in for the landing and seeing the tiny little houses, swimming pools, roadways, and miniature cars getting bigger and bigger the closer we got to the airport. You get a different perspective on life from that vantage point. I remember my brother looking out the airplane window and saying to mom, "Why are there snowdrifts down there?" My mom answered very politely that they weren't snowdrifts, but clouds. That astounded me! We were actually flying above the clouds. I thought at the time that we must be flying in heaven, but I didn't see any people. They must have had to get out of the way of the airplane. From that moment on I always loved to fly.

Sooner or later the good times have to end, but, thankfully, good memories last forever.

The year 1968 began a new period in my life. Oh, how I wanted to be included with the "in crowd" in junior high. They were the popular kids, extroverted and joyful. They were the cheerleaders, football players, basketball players, and majorettes. I constantly practiced cheerleading and baton twirling in my bedroom in front of the full-length mirror attached to the back of my bedroom door. If I practiced hard enough, just maybe I could make one of the squads, but I never did. My parents didn't seem that enthusiastic about whether or not I made the squad. In fact, on one occasion, my mother was so mad that I dropped the baton in the house she grabbed it from my hand and hit me on the palm with it. My dad immediately came to my defense, but that incident took the wind out of my sails. She was sorry after she did it. I want to emphasize that this outburst was a one-time incident and there was nothing dramatic in my childhood that would cause me to suddenly become depressed. No abuse, no alcoholism. I was just an ordinary, run-of-the-mill child who liked to play and have fun! I came from a "stereotypical family" and a small town.

We were happy, healthy children. My father had suffered from polio in the early days of my life, but fortunately he came out of it with no permanent side effects. My mother suffered daily, with only one lung, and had to have daily treatments on a slant board. She also had a weak heart and didn't always have the energy to do the things she wanted to do. As a child it was painful to watch her. It wasn't until forty years later that I realized that she probably suffered from another disease; one that people didn't talk about or admit to at that time, because of the stigma attached to it. The disease was undiagnosed depression. She never really seemed happy and she would blow up at times for little cause. Maybe it was her lung disease or maybe she truly suffered from clinical depression. I can only guess in retrospect.

Suicide

"The Lord is close to the brokenhearted and saves those who are crushed in spirit," (Psalm 34:18, NIV*).*

It wasn't until my high school years that I began to show the signs and symptoms of depression. I spent a tremendous amount of time in my bedroom studying, thinking, and daydreaming. I rarely came out. When my brother went off to college in 1970, I was devastated. Mark was excited about getting away from home and didn't seem to care that I was left behind. I probably would have felt the same way if I were in his shoes. He always helped me take some of the wrath from my mother. Now it would be mandatory for me to be strong and now I was forced to deal with everything myself. How was I ever going to make it?

The seclusion continued and was rarely questioned

until one day in September 1971, when I found myself in my bedroom and unable to breathe. I could barely get my parents' attention to let them know there was a problem. I was gasping for breath. What was happening to me? My chest was heaving as I was trying to suck in the air, but it wouldn't come. My chest became heavier until it felt as though it was in a vice that was slowly being cranked to a closed position. My dad tried artificial resuscitation while my mother called for an ambulance. The medics immediately starting giving me oxygen, but it didn't seem to help. I just kept gasping for breath and my hands, arms, legs, and feet became tingly and numb. I could hear the sirens on the ambulance and thought to myself, *this is serious.*

When I arrived at the hospital, after what seemed like an eternity, they determined I had been hyperventilating and they put a paper bag over my mouth and nose to allow me to get more carbon dioxide into my system. In psychological terms, this was my first panic attack. This would be one of many that I would experience over the years to come.

My life started spiraling out of control my junior year of high school. I was very introverted, and liked to keep to myself. Standing up in front of the class to give a speech or even answering a question in class felt as if someone were pulling my finger nails out. I not only felt that the class was snickering at me, but the teachers as well. Nevertheless, I still ended up getting a fair grade so I couldn't have done that badly. I would visibly shake and knew the entire class could see me. I could feel the classroom closing in and I would see their faces with grim smirks. I felt trapped in a body that I didn't recognize. How could I ever get over my fear? I didn't want to be like this; I wanted to be like I thought everyone else was: extroverted, calm, graceful, and outgoing.

During those years, I was slightly overweight and somewhat clumsy. I wasn't permitted to wear make-up, and we couldn't afford contact lenses at that time. My eyes were extremely nearsighted and the lenses in my glasses were thick and awkward. I was definitely not in the "in-crowd." I always felt I was on the outside looking in. Nevertheless, I was an excellent student with nothing but A's and B's on my report cards. As my high school years progressed, so did I, at least in the intellectual department. I was getting straight A's in my senior year, would be lettering in volleyball, and had a good chance at a local scholarship. I had everything going for me, yet something was terribly, terribly wrong.

I studied diligently every night, and when I was finished studying I stared at the walls in empty silence. My thoughts sometimes raced about thinking of school, church, and how I felt about myself, and then there were times when my mind was as blank as a white-washed wall. When I think back around that time, I don't really remember planning on killing myself. The thoughts just kept creeping into my mind ever so slowly.

Depression hurts from the depths of one's innermost soul. I don't remember where I had been or why I was there, but one night I was driving home on the bypass and turned off at my exit. There was a steep embankment on the other side, and I suddenly thought that I would roll the car over and over again and that would be the end. I wanted to die so badly. I hurt from the pit of my stomach. It was a spontaneous gesture with no planning involved. My heart felt as if it were being crushed. The deep dark hole had become deeper and darker, and there was no light in my life. Instead of taking the curve slowly and carefully as I was taught in driver's education, I gunned it, full-speed ahead, and I crashed into the guardrail, bouncing off it like a ping-pong ball. This was back when most cars didn't have seatbelts and the impact threw me across the full size front seat of the car and slammed me into the passenger door. The car came slowly to a stop while I tried to work my way back to the driver's side. *How disappointing,* I thought. I *don't even think I made a dent in the sturdy guardrail.* This was my first suicide attempt and I had failed miserably. My parents thought I had just lost control, and my dad never said a word as he pounded out the dents in the car. Neither my mom nor my dad showed any suspicion after the accident. They just thought I was going through the "teenage" years. Although the one curious thing about the car accident was that I was never punished for it. My mother was just thankful that I wasn't hurt.

I told a girlfriend that I had tried to kill myself that night, but she never told anyone else. She probably didn't take me seriously. I was depressed, and I believe my family finally began to notice but didn't seem concerned. It was a typical Christmas. We celebrated Christmas Eve at my grandparent's home and spent Christmas day at home unwrapping presents and enjoying a special meal. The year ended, and everyone welcomed 1973!

The holidays were over, winter had settled in, and my mind was tired and lifeless. I was feeling helpless to do anything to make my mom's life easier. With one lung she was always sick and it was difficult for her to breath at times. My dad had taken over the household chores and insisted that I concentrate on my studies. I missed my brother and wanted him to come back home from college. My self-esteem was at an all-time low, and a deep depression overtook me very quickly. It was as if the sky was always black. I never had any sunshine in my life and I never thought about turning to God for strength. My heart felt heavy, and I had lost interest in everything. The physical and psychological pain was beyond unbearable, and I wanted immediate relief of the most extreme kind. All I ever wanted to do was to sit in the seclusion of my room and daydream. This was my "safe" place where no one could see me or talk to me. I didn't have to wear a mask to please people. I was so despondent during what should have been the happiest time of my life - I was a senior in high school!

I had pre-planned that infamous day of my demise. I purchased a bottle of over-the-counter sleeping pills and locked it in a small, green tin safe in my room. I had gone through the medicine cabinet when no one was home to see if there were any other pills I could add to the mix. I found a nearly full bottle of prescription sleeping pills. This was perfect for me. I planned to kill myself on a Friday night, because I knew my parents were going to a doctor in Michigan and wouldn't be home until later that evening. I would be home alone with plenty of time for the pills to work.

It was a crisp, clear, sunny afternoon when I got home from school that day in early January 1973. I washed my face and combed my hair. I had worn my favorite outfit to school that day: my navy blue wool bell-bottomed pants and navy and beige plaid wool jacket. I was ready. I went to the kitchen, got a glass of water and methodically started swallowing all the pills. I didn't feel anything: not depression, confusion, anxiety, bitterness, nothing. I went into my bedroom, lay down on my bed, and waited to die.

Time stood still as I began to get drowsy. Many thoughts were swirling around in my head, yet I don't remember them. It was as if my mind was short-circuiting from the vast amount of medications it was absorbing. There were brief flashbacks. Thoughts of heaven, thoughts of hell, and the thought of what my mother and father would feel when they found me dead. My mind was cluttered and empty at the same time. What would my brother think?

My stomach churned with the mixture of pills and water and I drifted in and out of a semi-conscious sleep. This was something I needed to do. It would relieve me of the stress of not being perfect. It would take away the guilt and shame I felt in school and at home with my mother. No more studying, no more worries, no more cares or concerns.

Suddenly, I realized that maybe, just maybe, death wasn't the answer to my problems, whatever they were. Panic started to sink in. Then, for one brief second, my body jolted as if struck by a lightning bolt. It felt as if God had shaken the bed with all his might. God didn't want me to die! He wasn't ready for me yet.

I leaped out of bed and started to run for the telephone, but I didn't make it. I fell against the wall and collapsed into my brother's meticulous bedroom. *Oh dear heavenly Father, was I going to die*? My legs were numb, they wouldn't move. I tried to get up again and again, but my body wouldn't react. I tried crawling ever so slowly on my hands and knees. I don't remember how I finally made it to the black rotary telephone in the living room, but I decided to call my best friend at the time. She worked in a beauty shop in a nearby town and I knew she would be there. I don't remember dialing the number or what I said to her. All I know is that I was screaming uncontrollably into the phone. She told me to hang up the phone and she would get help. I hung up.

As I lay slumped on the hardwood floor by the telephone, I drifted off to sleep. Suddenly the front door burst open and my friend's dad bolted into the house. He owned a gas station just outside of Lakeside and had on greasy black pants and a blue shirt with his name embroidered on the left hand pocket.

He took one look at me and picked up the phone to call for an ambulance. He was trying to give me instructions on how to force myself to vomit. "Marla, put your finger down your throat! You have to vomit up the pills." I can briefly remember stumbling to the sink in the kitchen and sticking my finger down my throat. A few pieces of half-melted capsules came out of my mouth, but nothing more. I was tired, so tired. I had forgotten what he told me to do. He screamed at me to keep moving, try to vomit, walk, and move my arms, move my legs, to not lie down. I crawled to the couch, curled up into a ball, and fell into a delicate, peaceful sleep. I remember him continuing to yell, "Marla, get up! Marla, get up," but his voice was muffled and seemed far, far away. I just wanted to continue my peaceful sleep. I vaguely remember the rescue squad arriving, a single siren, and that was all, nothing but unconscious slumber.

When I awoke from my deadly sleep the following day, I was in a small single-bed hospital room. The walls were stark white, I had an IV in my arm, and I could hear voices coming from the hallway. My dad was sleeping in a chair at the foot of my hospital bed. He looked distraught even in his slumber. He had stayed with me all night. Maybe somebody loved me after all. He had been crying and seemed utterly confused and shocked. No one seemed to know this was coming. After all, in 1973, in a small town these things just didn't happen. Mental illness was only for those people in state institutions with padded cells. To outsiders this was just an accident. I didn't feel well and took too many pills, that was all. Young people, seventeen years of age, don't try to kill themselves. They're free, happy-go-lucky, and having fun. This was nothing more than a case of bad judgment. The majority of people in my small town would try to make it an accident, except family and friends that knew the truth.

The local hospital didn't have a psychiatrist or a psychiatric unit at the time, so I was transferred to St. Charles Hospital in Toledo, Ohio. This *disease* called clinical depression was, I thought, embarrassing to my parents. They had never experienced it in the family before (or just weren't saying). My parents initially complied with the doctor's orders and took the incident seriously. However, I don't think they agreed with everything the doctors were saying.

When I arrived at St. Charles Hospital, the staff was expecting me and immediately led me to a room that was to be my home for the next week. It had linoleum floors, three beds with ivory curtains between them, white walls, a couple of dresser drawers, and a few scattered armchairs. They asked my parents to leave and began giving me the grand tour. I was one of the youngest patients in the psychiatric ward at the time. Most were older, some even in their eighties. I noticed there were bars on the windows and all the doors to the outside of the ward were locked. I wasn't in a hospital, I was in prison. I felt hurt and betrayed at this point. I thought my parents were giving up on me just when I needed their love and acceptance. I needed someone to tell me they loved me and cared about me. What I was going through was scary because I didn't know what to expect. I couldn't help but think I had put myself in jail for the rest of my life. In essence, I did. I now had a *label.* It was called mental illness.

The medical therapy started almost at once. I was given a handful of pills to take, but told it was none of my business as to what they were for. After all, I was a minor. They would make me feel better. There were two community showers that were long and narrow with six showerheads. There was one for the men and one for the women. A game room next to the showers offered cards, board games, crossword puzzles, and numerous other attention-diverters. Then there was a large room where everyone ate together. The square wooden tables seated four and the chairs were solid wood and hard as a rock.

Pills were dispensed from a small nurses' station. It was all a blur to me once the pills started to kick in. All I could do was sleep. The nurses would wake me up for breakfast, I would eat a little, they would give me some pills, and I would go back to bed. The same happened for lunch and dinner. They struggled to get me up to play games and participate in other activities, but to no avail. The nurses finally gave up and told my doctor that I wouldn't cooperate. They scolded me continuously and made fun of me for not participating in an attempt to manipulate me to get out of bed.

I found out later that they were giving me antidepressants and muscle relaxers. The muscle relaxers were to help calm me down, but I don't know why they were giving them to me. I wasn't displaying anger or aggression. I was just so depressed. After one week the doctor told my parents that the hospital setting wasn't working for me, and he would only treat me as an outpatient. He took me off some of the medications and I was finally able to move around a little during the day. I don't remember how long I went to see him as an outpatient, but my parents finally agreed with me that the medication was not doing me any good, and neither was the doctor. The majority of the problem was that the doctor had me on far too much medication. I couldn't think two coherent thoughts in a row. My parents realized this and knew I wouldn't get better if I was a walking zombie. The doctor was belligerent and shocked that we wouldn't take his medical advice. I think he was used to treating older patients.

I stopped taking the pills and seemed to be getting my senses back. Mom and Dad hovered over me continuously and I can't say I blame them. My diagnosis had been severe clinical depression, and they already knew I was capable of covering up my true feelings. My life, however, continued on with me spending the majority of time in my bedroom. It was difficult to go back to school because I was not sure who did or did not know what I had tried to do. Fortunately, nobody mentioned anything. As for my parents, they swept it under the rug. No one ever asked, "Why did you do it?" It was to be kept a secret.

The rest of the school year was uneventful. I graduated in June 1973, third in my class, lettered in volleyball and earned a $200 scholarship from a local bank. Things were looking better and I got a job over the summer working at the Dock Shop in Lakeside where I waited on people, fixed hamburgers and fries and scooped ice cream for those enjoying the beautiful sunshine on the dock. The summer went by quickly, and it was now time to go off to college.

Matrimony

"Watch and pray so that you will not fall into temptation. The spirit is willing, but the body is weak," (Matthew 26:41, NIV*).*

August 1973 was the beginning of a different kind of life for me. I left home to begin pre-law classes at an out-of-state college. I was happy and eager to start a new journey. The summer had been great, the depression was gone, and life was looking up. As we pulled up to the dormitory that I would be staying in, I could only wonder what type of roommate I would have. I wondered, *would she be nice? Would we get along?* I had no need to worry because we bonded immediately. She was from New York and that was excitement in itself for a small-town girl. What exhilaration! I was away from home and on my own.

The dormitory I was living in had been a men's dormitory that had recently been turned into a women's dorm. The only thing that hadn't been converted was the bathrooms. When my roommate, Lori, and I walked into the restroom facilities, there were still urinals lined up against the wall. Some of the other women in the dorm decided that they weren't appealing to look at so they purchased pots of flowers to put in each urinal. It spruced up the place, but Lori and I laughed until we cried. It looked positively hysterical. The dorm rooms were pleasant with bunk beds, dresser drawers, and two tables. A large window looked out over the busy street below. The other side of the building faced the courtyard.

I was eager to start classes and meet my professors. College was more difficult from a homework point-of-view, but being able to go back to the dorm room and relax between classes was a nice perk. Things were going great. The depression had lifted over the summer and I finally felt free and relaxed again. It felt as if an enormous burden had been lifted off my shoulders.

I soon fell into my "perfectionist" mode and started studying non-stop. I ended up with a combination of A's and B's. Considering I had stayed up all night reading, writing, and studying for the final exams, I was thankful for the B's and didn't have my normal feelings of failure. Hallelujah! This was a major accomplishment for me.

Nevertheless, by the end of the semester, I had become homesick and was beginning to feel those old familiar thoughts of despair. I was definitely ready to go home for

Christmas. Unfortunately, the holidays brought only temporary relief before another semester began.

When I returned to college, I was shaky and unstable from the start. The dark side of depression was back and I lost all enthusiasm. I stayed in bed all day and never attended classes. This cloud of gloom brought with it a refusal to be cheered up. In fact, if anyone tried to cheer me up, I grudgingly summoned one of my ghostly smile masks then slid back into my pit of despair. I suffered from numerous panic attacks and after one week dropped out of school. It wasn't that I couldn't make the grades. I had proven to myself that I was intelligent and came through with A's and B's. It was the fact that my mind was dead and I felt it was impossible for me to accomplish any type of major goal. I was extremely tired. All I wanted to do was sleep.

After spending three months at home, mostly in bed, I decided to try again. I enrolled at a local college where I attended classes during the day and worked the switchboard at night. I turned my attention to earning a secretarial degree and the classes became much easier for me. I was actually beginning to enjoy life again. I had lost weight, purchased contact lenses, dressed in suits, and was highly respected. I realized much later that I was seeking and receiving people's approval rather then God's approval.

This also happened to be the same time that I met my first husband-to-be. We met on a blind date through a mutual friend. I was nervous because I had never dated in high school, but decided to push past the butterflies and go for it. His name was Ted and he was slightly shorter than I was. He was an ordinary fellow with dark brown hair and brown eyes with a manner that was so gentle and kind. We continued to date for a year and decided to get married.

We were married in June 1975. It was a small church wedding with friends and family. The reception was held in a local hall with a live band, great food, and a beautiful wedding cake. My depression had disappeared and life was good again. This man was the light of my life. I truly loved him.

We spent our honeymoon in Maine eating fresh lobster, oysters on the half shell, shrimp, and many other delicacies. We had many great times together. We both liked to go camping and canoeing at Mohican State Park, and we walked the numerous trails that were available. We watched people fly fish in the river with their deep wader pants on and half a dozen different flies hooked to their jackets.

Our marriage was financially shaky throughout the first few years. My husband was laid off and my meager salary at the college stretched our pocketbooks, but we were eager to see what life would bring. When he was called back to work, we were able to move out of our tiny one-bedroom apartment and buy a house in Sandusky, Ohio. Things were going great for five years and then, as predicted, came the urge to have a baby. I had difficulty conceiving, but after many doctor appointments and various treatments, I finally heard the words I'd been waiting to hear, "You're pregnant!" We were ecstatic. We were expecting our first child, and I was eager for all the hustle and bustle to begin. *What were we going to name him or her? What did we need to do first*? Let's see ... we needed a crib, clothes, car seat, bibs, diapers, a changing table–the list went on. It was a wonderful two weeks.

Yes, I said two weeks. What was supposed to be a glorious, radiant occasion quickly turned into a nightmare. I vomited morning, noon, and night throughout the pregnancy. I was hospitalized too many times to count and lived on IVs, Visteril shots, Benedictine, coke syrup, and dry baked potatoes for the following eight months! While in the hospital, my chart clearly stated that I was allergic to codeine. When I had a serious migraine they promised to get me something for it. They gave me codeine and I almost lost the baby. That taught me to ask questions next time.

When the big day finally arrived, I was ready. My water broke at 6:00 a.m. and Steven Christopher Chudy was born at 9:01 a.m. He was so precious and, thankfully, healthy, even with all the medications I'd had to take. What a beautiful bundle of joy. We were all so happy.

I soon found that a baby is not easy to take care of, especially in the early years. I wanted to do everything right and was terrified I'd do something wrong. Steven was colicky and up most of the night. Being the perfectionist I was, I would stay up all night with him and then when he slept during the day in his carrier, I rocked the carrier with my foot while washing the dishes. I spent the day scrubbing floors, dusting, and generally trying to keep the house in order. Once again the heart started to palpitate, the stomach hurt, the mind went blank, and the demon came back. I felt guilt, pain, and insecurity. I felt anxious and unworthy. I was not prepared for the responsibility of taking care of a baby even though I was twenty-five years old. The warmth, joy, and excitement vanished.

After telling my doctor I couldn't take it anymore and wanted to kill myself, I was immediately hospitalized in our local psychiatric ward and diagnosed with post-partum depression. I was, once again, started on a regimen of antidepressants. I was hospitalized for more than a month before my doctor felt I was strong enough to return home. Even then it was only because I put on my smiley face mask and said what I knew he wanted to hear.

The mask stayed on. I went back to work full-time and was totally disenchanted with life. Ted was laid off again so caring for the baby and the house became a second full-time job. My husband was suffering from his own depression at this time, and together we didn't have the strength or ability to help each other.

With the pressure of my job and the pressure at home, I needed someone to love me and understand what I was going through. I met a man in the office where I worked during that time and we felt an instant hidden attraction for each other. We both let it go for months and then started staying late after work in order to talk. He was sympathetic and kind. He understood me and was able to comfort me.

One night he asked if I'd like to meet him somewhere. I thought he meant a restaurant, but he had other plans. He stopped his car on a back country road and had me get into the backseat. This was my first and only *affair*.

I felt good because I thought I was getting the love and attention that I needed so badly, but at the same time I felt extreme guilt, condemnation, and deep grief. Here I was with a wonderful husband and beautiful baby son at home, and I was in the backseat of a car with a man I barely knew. There was no romance, no love, no butterflies, no compassion, just lust on his part and need on my part. *What was I thinking?* I had just broken one of the Ten Commandments. *Would God ever be able to forgive me, or was I going straight to hell?*

The guilt was more than I could bear. I finally confessed the affair to my husband, who was shocked and hurt. My mind was in a whirlwind. I was hurting, confused, ashamed, embarrassed, and guilty, struggling to search for words that would make it better, but there were none. I knew my husband was hurting. He loved me and trusted me. I searched for the answers as to how I could possibly do this to him. The future would hold the answer. I felt that I had missed something in my life, since I had gone from living with my parents to living with my husband. I yearned for the right to be on my own and do my own thing. This led to my belief that the marriage was dead. I wondered, *how would my husband ever be able to trust me again?*

I felt terrible and knew I needed God in my life. On March 18, 1982, I wrote in the back of my small, green Gideon Bible that I accepted the Lord Jesus Christ as my personal Savior. In that same year, when Steven was two years old, I asked for a divorce. This totally devastated my husband and diminished my faith. He was such a wonderful husband. How could I possible hurt someone that I loved so badly?

I moved into a somewhat dilapidated trailer and called it home. My brother and father helped me to renovate the inside and conquer the surrounding chest-high grass that required a sickle before it could even be mowed. They tore out the built-in dresser drawers to accommodate my bedroom set. My mom and I painted the bathroom, and I had new carpeting installed in Steven's room. I had received custody of Steven in the divorce.

I finally had just what I yearned for: the freedom of owning my own place, a good job, and a wonderful son. What more could I ask for? Party time! When my ex-husband had Steven for a weekend, it was time to party. A couple of my co-workers smoked marijuana and asked me if I wanted to try some. Of course I said "yes." After all, Steven was safely in his father's care, and I was free! The feeling was so light and airy, and I didn't have a care in the world. This was something I had never felt before. I began to purchase my own drugs and smoke more and more when I was home alone. I even rolled my own marijuana cigarettes and had a party at the trailer one night and made marijuana brownies for dessert. I then began to add alcohol to the already tenuous situation, and my problems became a blur. After all, I was still on antidepressants from my post-partum depression. The mixture of drugs, alcohol, and antidepressants made me carefree and I wasn't eating properly. There were many nights when all I would have for supper was a bowl of cereal. I kept losing weight and came very close to becoming anorexic. I then had the opportunity to try cocaine. Some friends of mine (and I use the term loosely) were going to have a party and invited me over. They said the cost of cocaine was fifty dollars. I was weak and hungry for friends, so I saved up the money and was ready to go when they suddenly cancelled the plans. I thank God for his intervention. For some reason, the opportunity never presented itself again. If it had, I would probably have thought twice about it, but God intervened and the plans fell through.

The depression deepened, and since I didn't care for my psychiatrist at the time, I went to my family doctor. He really didn't know what to do about severe depression. While he was attending other patients, trying to decide what to do with me, I ran out of the office. He called me at home and told me he wanted to admit me to the psychiatric ward. I thought to myself, *not again*. He finally agreed to admit me to the medical ward for the night, but I had to agree to see a psychiatrist in the morning. I submitted to his request and ended up in the psychiatric ward the following day. This time it was a round of new antidepressants and anti-anxiety medications. I felt as though I was on a roller-coaster ride and couldn't get off. I was put on Elavil (an antidepressant) and Ativan (a tranquilizer). I was in the hospital for weeks until I received a call from my employer telling me to, "Get my act together and get back to work." Once again I put on my smiley face mask and said exactly what I knew the doctor wanted to hear. I was out, and within three days back to work. After a while you learn what the doctors want to hear. You tell them you're feeling better and the medication must be working. They always like it when they are right about the medication(s). Next, you start playing the nurses. You participate in activities, initiate activities, become friendly with them, and tell everyone how much better you're feeling. Nurses write everything down, so don't overdo it.

As time went on, I found it more difficult to take care of my son. I transferred legal custody to my ex-husband and started paying child support. It was the best decision I could have made for my son, considering the circumstances. I was unable to give him the attention and proper care that he needed because I was too messed up.

Then, in May of 1986, I met my second husband-to-be. We were in a singing group together and he asked me out on a date. We had a surprising attraction for each other and the relationship blossomed quickly. I stopped using marijuana, because I didn't want him to know about it, plus I had already started to give it up, and one month later, we were married and off to Mexico for our honeymoon. I looked in the bathroom mirror on the morning we were married and asked myself, *why am I doing this? I don't love him.* However, the need for companionship overwhelmed me and I ended up saying, "I do" when I really wanted to say, "I don't." I wondered, *why was I so weak and confused? What on earth was I thinking? Was this the depression playing games with my mind?*

I knew on the honeymoon that I had made a mistake. We were coming back from Mexico and going through customs when he jokingly said, "I hope they don't find all the drugs in our suitcase." He was joking, of course. We didn't have any drugs in our suitcases, but I was aware of the consequences of even making a statement like that, just from reading the newspapers. I was furious at the fact of how immature he was!

After we were married and the honeymoon was over, he got another job and we moved to southern Ohio. This meant being away from my son and getting adjusted to a new town, a new job, and playing the part of the "perfect wife" of a band director. I spent my time kissing up to administrative school officials where my husband was teaching. I attended every football game, basketball game, and concert. I even became the announcer for the marching band. My reward was the band members throwing spitballs at me during the games. I kept thinking, *there were some good times, but where are they now?*

Two years later my husband decided to take a job closer to our earlier home, and we were able to move back to Sandusky. We found a beautiful brick home with hardwood floors, a full basement, a first floor that included a lovely, sunny breakfast nook, a second floor with three bedrooms and a bath, and a fully finished attic. It was huge, but my husband wanted it and his enthusiasm finally rubbed off on me. We signed the papers in October to purchase the house, and my husband quit his job in December of that same year. He decided to work as an insurance salesman, but it wasn't a job that he was suited for so things didn't work out. The stress and tension mounted and, even though we tried marriage counseling, it didn't work. Here was another marriage down the tubes and one more failure to add to my trophy case. I wondered to myself, *Now what was God going to think about me? He surely couldn't love me after this. Why was I giving up so easily?* I needed to work at having a good marriage, but I didn't have the strength of mind to do it anymore. My disease was taking over my life.

This time I moved into a tiny, one-bedroom apartment. I was depressed and lonely. I felt numb inside and felt that God had abandoned me because I was such a bad person. My parents weren't extremely happy with me at this point in my life, and the move only added to the intensity. I had a sewing chair that had a seat I could lift up and store sewing materials in. It was a rather meaningless chair and I wasn't being too careful with it. When it came out of the moving van and I started carrying it into the apartment the seat came off, the chair dropped, and everything in it went flying. That was just enough to push me over the edge. I sat down in the middle of the living room floor and began to sob uncontrollably with no consolation from anyone. When the move was complete and everyone was gone, I sat in the living room with boxes all around me, popped a few extra antidepressants, and washed them down with alcohol. The depression was so intense the tears wouldn't stop flowing. I thought, *my second marriage had only lasted four years. What was my problem?*

I went to work the following Monday with swollen, red eyes. The grief and guilt over my many failures was taking its toll. The depression kept getting deeper and deeper as if my life were being slowly snuffed out. The intensity of depression cuts so deep and so far, it is difficult to imagine.

In January 1990, with the divorce proceeding slowly, the pressure was too great. I swallowed a bottle of Elavil (my antidepressant) and started drinking. I didn't want to live, I wanted to die. I called a friend to talk, but she must have heard the slur of my words and came over to check on me. She later told me that I was unconscious by the time she arrived and I couldn't be revived. She called an ambulance and I was rushed to the hospital. I woke up in the intensive care unit of our local hospital the following day, after having my stomach pumped. There was a tube down my throat, an IV in my arm, and heart and blood pressure monitors all over the place. The tube was causing me to choke, so I pulled it out. Along with the tube came what seemed like a massive amount of blood. I called the nurse and she came in and actually cursed me for pulling out the tube. She said the doctor would probably have to put it back down my throat. I couldn't speak but thought to myself, *just let him try*.

I was bitter that I had not managed to kill myself, and it started coming out in fits of anger and aggression. Once again, I ended up back in the psychiatric ward. By this time they recognized my name, and greeted me as if I were an old friend. It's daunting when the psychiatric ward and your pharmacist know you by your first name. I spent weeks in the psychiatric unit. During that time my doctor was trying one medication after another. Nothing seemed to work. Elavil obviously didn't work anymore, since I used it to try to kill myself, so they had to find another medication. After numerous trials and errors my doctor finally found one he thought would work. I was put on Pamelor and then officially diagnosed with severe, recurrent, clinical depression, and thrown back out into the cold, cruel world to cope. Once again, my suicide attempt was swept under the rug with no one asking, "Why?" By this time, all I wanted to do was get physically sick. I wished for a more visible physical illness that people would understand.

Painful Days

"Turn from evil and do good; seek peace and pursue it," (Psalm 34:14, NIV*).*

This is the chapter that was the most difficult to write about. It's also the reason it's the shortest chapter in the book. I'm ashamed at some of the things I did. It was only years later that I would learn that a different disease was causing the chemical imbalances in my brain. I was already familiar with terms such as serotonin, dopamine, and norepinephrine. They are chemicals in the brain that affect mood. Selective serotonin re-uptake inhibitors (SSRI's, type of antidepressant), benzodiazepines (tranquilizers such as Valium and Xanax), Tricyclics (antidepressants such as Elavil), and electroconvulsive therapy (ECT) were part of my vocabulary. Later, words like Lithium, Abilify,

Lamictal, mood stabilizers, and anti-psychotics would be added to my list of medical terminology.

This period in my life was, thankfully, short-lived, but it was also the worst. I was on antidepressants and anti-anxiety medication at the time and turned to alcohol for relief. When I drank, I lost all my inhibitions. I became promiscuous and uninhibited. I would say whatever I wanted to say and I craved the attention that I received on the dance floor. My weight was down to 120 pounds and I am five feet nine inches tall, my blond hair was long and flowing, my blue contact lenses enhanced my eyes, and I loved every minute of it. I was the one person everyone wanted for a one-night stand! The guy on the dance floor, the used car salesman, the bartender, the factory worker, the self-employed, the unemployed, the executive, the attorney, the college professor—males from all walks of life. It didn't matter. I was searching for answers in all the wrong places. I felt so alone.

To be honest, I never enjoyed the sex, but the closeness made me feel loved and accepted. I was carefree and didn't realize that my life was rolling downhill like a big, white snowball in the dead of winter, gaining strength and momentum. Once again hopelessness began to surround me like thick morning fog.

I kept asking, "God, where are you?" However, I was too distraught to hear him tell me, in his soft, warm voice, that he was right beside me.

This was not the little girl from a small town in northern Ohio. It was a mask: the hair, the clothes, the eyes, the make-up—nothing but a mask that I would put on when I got up in the morning. I could be whatever anyone wanted me to be. All I had to do was reach into my magic bag and pull out a mask to fit the occasion. As soon as I put on the mask, the depression would no longer show on my face. People liked me and I was accepted. The high school "geek" was gone and an alternate personality took over. The truth was, I hated myself. I wanted everything to stop. I wanted to ask God for forgiveness, but I didn't know how. I thought to myself, *besides, how would he ever be able to forgive me?*

It was during this time period that I started dating my third husband-to-be. We met through a mutual friend of his that I had been dating. It didn't work out with his friend because he was forty-seven years old and intent on having a baby. I knew this definitely wasn't for me so I had a talk with him. We ended up going our separate ways. I started dating my third husband-to-be and my old boyfriend found someone new. They were married and had a beautiful baby girl. Ironically we all ended up as great friends and had each other over for dinner.

The new man in my life was a handsome man with a good job, a somewhat arrogant personality, and a sailboat. His dream was to one day sail around the world. It sounded romantic at the time. It also sounded like a pipe dream, but I admired his courage in wanting to do something so dangerous and yet exotic.

I had limited experience with sailing, but knew enough to barely get me by. He was going to teach me everything I needed to know, from the bow to the stern. I learned to duck when we "came about" so I wouldn't get clobbered by the boom. I learned about halyards, berths, lines (not ropes), portholes, heads, and bulkheads. I learned how to operate the radio and the GPS navigation system, how to plot courses, read depth sounders, and when to "give way." Hundreds of terms were swimming around in my head. It was a new life on water! I soaked it all up, made new friends, and wore sailing tee shirts. I didn't really enjoy sailing, but it was something my husband enjoyed, so I went along with the idea.

In order to learn more, I took Power Squadron courses. Basic boating, seamanship, piloting, and advanced piloting—it was a challenge. Yet, in the back of my mind, I knew I was doing it all for him, not for me. Was I about to head down another path to destruction?

Why did I keep on trying to be what everyone else wanted me to be? Why couldn't I just be me? Insecurity, the need for acceptance, hopelessness, depression; they all fought to eat away a slice of my brain and leave me in bondage to Satan. The feelings were devastating!

On The Water

"For *everything that was written in the past was written to teach us, so that through endurance and the encouragement of the scriptures we might have hope," (Romans* 15:4, NIV*).*

I was still suffering from depression and was now taking Prozac. It was my little, green and white wonder drug–the flavor of the year. I was also taking medication for migraines that seemed to be occurring more and more frequently. Maybe that should have told me something.

I really loved my third husband-to-be and didn't understand it when I found him sleeping with another woman during our courtship. It broke my heart. I couldn't understand what was happening. Did he love me or not? That was it. I was through with men. Forget it—what a waste of precious time! We weren't even married yet, and already I couldn't trust him.

We broke up for several weeks and I honestly thought I would never hear from him again. I certainly didn't want to. Then, just as I was leaving work one day, my phone rang. I hesitated to pick it up. I was ready to go home and it was probably someone who needed lengthy information about something or other. However, my work ethic kicked in and I went back to answer it. In retrospect, I wish I never had. It was him and he wanted to "talk." He asked if he could come over that night. The minute I heard his voice, my heart melted into a giant puddle of water. "Yes," I said. "Just give me a chance to get home."

I don't know what I expected—an apology, begging for forgiveness, saying it was all a big mistake, and that he'd never do it again. Wow, was I ever wrong! He didn't apologize; he didn't beg for forgiveness, he didn't say it was a mistake, and that he'd never do it again. He said, "She seduced me."

"What! She seduced you! Does that make things better?" I screamed. I knew what the truth really was, but I wouldn't admit it to anyone. The reality was he only wanted me back because I was the only one willing to take off and sail around the world with him. I knew this was going to be another mistake. I kept asking myself, *what am I doing?* However, my insecurities and need for love and companionship overtook the practical part of me—if there was a practical part.

Nevertheless, even with the knowledge and gut feelings that I had, I took him back. I loved him despite his faults and besides, I had plenty of my own faults lurking in the closet. I reached beyond my gut feeling and took him back. The old saying that "love is blind" rings true.

When he asked me to marry him, I accepted with the understanding that we wouldn't depart on the cruise for another year and a half. He agreed and we went to look at wedding rings. He picked out a plain gold band for $45 and said, "Let's go." My thoughts were swirling. Why didn't he let me have some input into the decision about the ring? I was right there and yet felt left out. It hurt! I felt as if my thoughts and opinions didn't count.

We were married on October 6, 1993. He quit his lucrative job in December of that same year without informing me about his decision to do so. This was all too familiar with my last marriage when my husband suddenly decided to quit his job just after we purchased a house. I believed a man and wife should talk over something like quitting a job. It's a major decision, and once again I felt angry and betrayed. Why couldn't he have consulted me? What if I had done something like that to him?

In April he informed me that we would be leaving on our "trip" in June! I didn't want to leave that soon. He had agreed to wait until the following year. I questioned, *what was happening? The Bible says that the wife is supposed to obey her husband, but this was unfair. Why were things going so wrong?* I felt shock, disbelief, fear, and apprehension. If I were to write a book strictly about the boat trip, I would title it *Mixed Emotions: the Sea of Uncertainty*. My stomach churned, and I felt angry and betrayed. This just wasn't right. I wondered, *why didn't he care what I thought? What about my feelings?* His response to me was, "You're just insecure, and you need to grow up!" He was right that I was insecure, but if I would have grown up, the relationship would have ended right then and there.

The planning continued and my heart kept screaming, "No, no." But, once again, I wanted to please everyone. I had been taught not to make waves. Besides, he had made up his mind to go and would have gone by himself at the drop of a hat. I certainly couldn't stomach the possibility of a third failed marriage, so I went along with the plans he was making.

I quit my job in May and sold everything I owned, including my cute little 1991 teal Ford Escort GT. It had a manual transmission and was really fun to drive. I even gave away my work clothes and black leather pumps. I just kept thinking, *this couldn't be God's will for my life, could it?* I cried myself to sleep each night as my depression, once again, started coming at me with gale force winds. I asked, *why weren't the medications working?* I had tried just about everything on the market.

It was decided that my son, Steven, and a friend of his would go along for the first leg of the journey. I loved my son, and even though I didn't have custody, my first husband was very understanding about letting him go along. That was as long as he was back in time for school in the Fall. It seems strange not to have mentioned my son before this. He was a very important part of my life. He loved it when just the two of us would do something special together, but when any of my husbands were involved, he hated it with a passion. He wanted me all to myself, and to tell you the truth, I wanted him all to myself. I wanted Steven to go on this trip. I thought it would be an enjoyable experience for him, but I didn't want him to go just because he wanted to please me.

The boys were on the boat and we were ready to go the following day. However, at 3:00 in the morning, Steven's friend woke us up to tell us Steven had run away because he didn't want to go. After fifteen minutes of frantically searching the marina area, I decided he had probably gone to his grandmother and grandfather's house. We drove slowly to see if we could find him but didn't see him anywhere. When we arrived at his grandparents' house, he was there crying. I sat down with him and asked for some privacy, only to discover he hated my husband and did not want to go on the trip. I felt so sorry for him, that he couldn't tell me earlier. I assured him it was all right, and he didn't have to go on the boat. I wouldn't be upset at all. This seemed to calm him down and make it more bearable for both of us.

So the journey started out on Wednesday, July 7, 1994, with no Steven or friend. We said good-bye to our friends and attempted to start the engine. No luck. This marvelous machine that had never given us grief before was suddenly balking at the idea of having to motor down 2,000 miles of rivers. Whatever the case, a black cloud seemed to be following us. I believe that God was trying to tell me not to go and giving me numerous opportunities to back out, but I didn't have enough wisdom to listen to him.

Once the motor was repaired, we began our journey. Three days out and our troubles began. The forecast called for waves to approximately three feet with winds to clock around to ninety degrees. This would give us a nice beam reach sail, the best. About two hours out of the harbor, we realized this wasn't going to happen. Conditions deteriorated quickly.

We decided that since it would take us another two and one-half hours to get back to our starting point, we decided to continue. They say all sailors make bad decisions, and this was one of our winners! We spent a total of ten hours beating into waves averaging eight to ten feet high. My stomach didn't like the coffee and dry cereal being tossed around like lottery balls in a blowing machine, and it rebelled. I couldn't even think about going below. Even in my long winter underwear, 100% wool Ireland sweater, and full foul weather gear I still felt chilled to the bone. My husband and I were taking turns at the helm. While one person was at the helm, the other could get up under the dodger and out of the wind. It almost felt better for me to be at the helm steering. It made me concentrate and kept my mind off my flopping stomach. I was at the helm better than halfway through our voyage when I saw the wave coming. It was like slow motion—building up to a massive climax when it peaked. In the next instant, I was no longer sitting at the helm in my comfortable motorboat seat, but rather feeling the sharp pain of the rail, on the side of the cockpit, in the center of my spine. I lay there for a minute grimacing in pain. All I wanted to do was to wake up and realize this was all just a bad dream, that I had never married him or agreed to go on this trip. However, it was not a dream and the reality of the pain made me realize that I hated sailing.

We finally made it to the next marina where we discovered a few problems. We had taken in water through the chain locker, which resulted in approximately thirty to forty gallons in the bow of the boat. Also, the forward hatch had not been fully secured and all our clothes were wet. There was water in the bilge and the navigation station was saturated. And this was just the beginning of the trip. I hope the rest of our journey went better than this!

The sailing continued. I knew early on that I had made a promise to sail around the world that I could not keep. I also realized that my husband didn't seem as anxious to, "sail around the world," as he had earlier. I don't believe either one of us had the skills required doing something like that, at least I know I didn't, and the experiences weren't getting any easier.

As we were leaving one of the many ports we stayed in on Lake Michigan, the current caught the back end of the boat and forced the bow into a dock pole, breaking off the port (left) running light. The captain was not happy because this meant another repair job that needed to be done. The light was finally repaired in South Haven, Michigan, after spending days waiting on parts. A few days after it was repaired, we were leaving our dock in Michigan City. We were concerned with getting out of the dock because of the strong winds that were persisting. We found out that we were concerned for good reason. The port running light that had just been repaired needed to be repaired again. As we were leaving the dock, the bow line got snagged on one of the wooden dock poles. I was worried that it wouldn't pull loose, and my full attention was devoted to trying to free it. Well, much to my husband's chagrin, it freed itself at about the same time the port running light was detaching itself from its somewhat precarious location on the bow sprint.

I was seriously considering building a metal cage around it (like the bars they put on jailhouse windows). The light seemed so vulnerable. I wondered, *why don't boat manufacturers think of things like that?* Since this was the second time in a row this had happened, it struck me as being funny and I couldn't stop laughing! The captain was furious. He screamed obscenities at me, and at one point started heading towards the bow of the boat with a frightening look on his face. At that moment, I feared for my life. This was ironic, considering I had tried to kill myself three times. I was just about to jump overboard into the icy, cold water, when he suddenly realized he needed to be at the helm steering the boat. I hadn't considered the mishap as being anyone's fault. It was just an accident, but it was obvious my husband didn't see it that way. The captain finally calmed down, but the day's journey was still emotionally uncomfortable.

We finally came to the river system and started heading south. I was still on Prozac at this time, and when we got farther down the river system, I ran out of my medication. I wanted to get to a pharmacy so they could call my doctor and get me a new prescription, but my husband informed me I would have to wait. Once again he had the last word, but this was a bad decision on his part. I slowly began to feel the intensity of my depression increase. By the time we got to Mobile, Alabama, I was lifeless, depressed, and suffering from what I thought was an eye infection.

A couple of days later I realized I needed to get to a doctor for my eye. We called a cab to get to a local clinic. The area seemed questionable at first, but the clinic was large, well organized, and clean. After putting dye in my eye and looking at it under a black light, the doctor informed me I had scratched the cornea, which is very painful. They rinsed the eye with a pain killer/cleansing solution seven times, then put antibiotic drops in it, and patched it. The doctor said that it was imperative that he check it again the next day. If it had started to heal sufficiently, he would give me another three days worth of antibiotic drops, take the patch off, and we could be on our way. While I was there I explained to him the situation with my Prozac. With no questions asked, he gave me a huge bag of samples he had.

The next day I went back to the doctor, and after examining my eye, he felt that we could continue our sail. He gave me another three days worth of antibiotic drops and said I could take off the patch. This was good, because my husband was eager to get underway. I was secretly hoping that it would keep us there a few more days. I wasn't quite ready to get back on the water again.

After we left Mobile, Alabama, we headed toward Lake Pontchartrain to see New Orleans. We spent the night in the mangroves just outside of Lake Pontchartrain, and my husband's anger reared its ugly head. I believed he was anchoring too close to another boat (there was plenty of room in the anchorage), and he felt I should mind my own business. After all, he was the captain. I mumbled something under my breath, and he started yelling obscenities at me. I had a strong feeling he would have come back and hit me had we not been so busy anchoring. A gentleman on the boat he was anchoring so near to also mentioned the distance between our boats, and my husband didn't spare his feelings either.

It was then that I realized my "job" on the boat was to keep my husband happy. He ran the ship and said where we were going, when we were going, and what we were going to do when we got there. If I hinted that I wanted to take a breather, he would push on in spite of my feelings. He wanted sex three times a day, and if he wasn't getting it, he took it. I had mixed feelings. It was difficult to perform when I didn't want to, although I believed it was my duty as a wife. *Duty* seems like such a harsh word, but in reality, I wasn't getting anything out of it, and I didn't enjoy it. It was a duty! In fact, I hated every minute of it and faked it every time. I felt dead when it came to the area of the bedroom. I felt I was being used. I thought marriage was a two-way street and that decisions were supposed to be made together, but I realized this wasn't happening. Things weren't right. In fact, they were eerily wrong. It was a long, uphill battle, and I was depressed and running out of energy, patience, and sanity—all this, with the worse yet to come.

Our next adventure took us from the Turks & Caicos to Luperon in the Dominican Republic. We left the Turks & Caicos with sunny skies and a stiff breeze, but by late afternoon the ocean swells were averaging ten to fifteen feet, the boat was riding like a bucking bronco, and once again, I thought to myself, *why am I doing this?* I guess it was the combination of large powerful swells, relentlessly high winds, and a twenty-four hour, pounding ocean passage, but my nerves were raw. For the first time, I honestly felt fear, or maybe apprehension would be a better word. It must have been the pitch black of night and unseen cresting waves that caused it to be more than I had prepared for. This was different from Lake Erie, different from the Gulf of Mexico, different from the Gulf Stream crossing. This was open ocean with no bottom!

The boat was being tossed around like a leaf in a bubbling Jacuzzi. Dishes were flying, bottles were rolling, and everything that wasn't tied down, bolted down, or glued into place was rattling, clanging, and banging. I cringed at the thought of broken dishes and smashed bottles. All this and we still had another ten hours to go! I couldn't help but wonder, *was I going to survive?*

As soon as the sun peeked above the horizon we headed toward the breath-taking view of the mountainous Dominican Republic. After twenty-four hours of hard-core sailing, we were less than two miles from the entrance of Luperon harbor. Once we were safely in the harbor, we maneuvered the boat to the customs dock, and tied up.

Customs and Immigration was our first truly educational experience with the Dominican Republic. We had no sooner docked when three customs agents boarded our boat, with sub-machine guns in hand, to ask questions and fill out paperwork. At this point I wanted to scream out, "Take the boat, take the husband, take it all and just let me go home!" Nevertheless, I kept my mouth shut and the procedure was relatively painless. They required a $10 entry fee and a bottle of Coca Cola as a tip. My husband paid the tip, to my surprise. Normally he would argue with them. Our voyage continued on, and as the sun started to rise, we saw the beautiful mountains of Guadeloupe. This would be a nice place to spend a few days and catch our breath.

A boat we were traveling with was having fuel filter

problems, so we decided to go into the first harbor we came to, rather than head on to Iles Des Saintes. We followed them into a crevice of a mountain known as Deshaies.

Despite my frustration with not making it to Iles Des Saintes, Deshaies (pronounced Day-hay), brought back my good spirits. It was a well protected bay surrounded by hills and mountains, together with the charming picturesque village built right on the beach. It was one of my favorite anchorages. The bright red roof tops looked like bulbs on a Christmas tree, in the midst of vivid green hillsides. Large palm trees dotted the white sand beach, along with wooden rowboats pulled up on shore.

We headed out the next day, my 40th birthday, and arrived in Iles Des Saintes within six hours. It was hot and sticky and everyone decided to go swimming. For some reason, the peace and tranquility that I had experienced the previous day had left me, and now I was suddenly in a powerful and sickening depression. The change happened so quickly it astonished me. As I swam around the harbor by myself, the tears would not stop flowing. I was having very strong thoughts of suicide at this point and wondered if my husband would even miss me. "Oh God, help me," I cried.

We spent the afternoon swimming, and then attended a big birthday bash later that night, hosted by another boat in the anchorage. Everyone brought a dish, and the host made a cheesecake complete with candles. I, once again, put on my best "smiley face" mask, and pretended to have a wonderful time; after all it was my birthday, and everyone would have been disappointed in me if I had acted like I felt inside.

We continued our journey to Trinidad, in the West Indies, in order to get the boat on land, get her repainted, and overhauled. This would give us time to return to the United States for the holidays. I was grateful to be heading back to the States. I was surprised to be thinking this, but I yearned for cuddling up in a blanket and watching snowflakes fall from the sky. It was so unbearably hot in Trinidad, that the thought of having to put on a sweater actually sounded appealing.

I missed my son and my family, and I despised the boat. I was in a hole, and I was being buried alive by depression. I had become acutely aware that this wasn't the right relationship for me to be in. I was being emotionally abused, and it was time for me to come under the authority of God, and listen to his voice of wisdom. I was ashamed that my third marriage was going to be a blunder. Satan hopes that shame will make us hang our heads and hide. There in the dark closet of secrecy, he wants to rob us of our dignity, and make us feel useless. Even though my emotions were highly negative, and I felt unworthy of God's love at the time, I knew that the Bible said God would never leave me nor forsake me, and I had to put my trust in him. I didn't want to come back to the boat ever again. We left Trinidad on November 8,

1995, via airplane. My heart was heavy and I didn't know what I wanted to do. The mental anguish was unbearable. I questioned, *what was going to happen to my marriage? Why was my depression not getting better?* Only God had the answers to my questions. I thought, *Call on God, Marla, call on God.*

Freedom at a Price

"So if the Son sets you free, you will be free indeed," (John 8:36 NIV*)*

Finally, we were home for the holidays. I was so grateful to be home, and was surprised when my depression hadn't lifted after a few days. In fact, it began to deepen. My medication wasn't working, and once again, I was beginning to have thoughts of suicide. It wasn't just the boat that was bringing me down; I was allowing my domineering husband to bring me down as well. I wondered, Was *it just the disease of depression rearing its ugly head?* I had already made up my mind before we left Trinidad that I was not going to return to the boat, and I was horrified as to how my husband was going to react.

During the short span of time that we were suppose to be in the States, my husband demanded that I get a job to earn some money for the trip, and he was ready and waiting for paydays. This afforded me the opportunity to start getting my life in order: deciding what to do, when to tell him that I wouldn't be returning to the boat, when to tell him I wanted a divorce. I was ashamed of getting another divorce, but I realized things were getting worse, and I had become fearful of my husband's temper. It was also time to tell my parents the situation. I found the time to let them know what was happening. I told them about my husband's anger, I told them about not going back to the boat, and I told them about the divorce. Wow! That must have been a shock to them after all the glorious newsletters I had written monthly to them. Gratefully, my parents were very supportive and the conversation went very well. My mother helped me cash checks and put money aside. My father thought my husband wasn't mechanical enough to be running a boat anyway and was delighted to hear I wouldn't be going back. They were elated that I would be home with my son, Steven. I also told them about my idea to take my husband to his sister's house and tell him there. That idea they bulked at. I would be alone without anyone to help me if things started going sour.

We had a trip planned out-of-state to see my husband's relatives, and we would be driving my parents' car. I decided to hold onto the keys so I could make a fast getaway, if necessary. I would tell him when we got there that I was not going back to the boat. This way he would have the support of his family. Bad idea! Things don't always work out as planned, and what may seem like a good idea at the time could turn out disastrous. I thought, *when was I going to start putting things into God's hands?* I believed in God and that his son, Jesus Christ, died on the cross for my sins. But this would be my third divorce. How much was he willing to forgive? The only common denominator in my three marriages was me and my illness. The shame and anguish was almost too much to bear.

After we arrived at his sister's business, we emptied the car and went through the usual chit-chat. My husband said he had forgotten something in the car, and wanted the keys. I said I would get it, but he got visibly angry, and demanded the keys. I relinquished them. After he returned, I asked his sister if I could speak to her alone. I thought that if she knew ahead of time that I wasn't going back to the boat, she could help soften the blow. We went upstairs to a conference room, and I informed her of my decision. I expected this to be a quiet, calm discussion, but instead, she flew into a rage. Before I even made it down the stairs, she raced down and told him that I was not going back to the boat with him. She started screaming at me and my husband went ballistic! He was kicking in the file cabinet, pounding his fists on the desk, and screaming obscenities. It was so loud that even some of the guys from the shop floor came in to see what was going on.

Unfortunately, I ended up across the room, with my husband and his sister between me and the door. In addition, he still had the keys to my parents' car. I kept asking him for the keys over and over again, and feared that he would assault me. Finally, he threw the keys as hard as he could. I put up my arm so they wouldn't hit my face, and they bounced off my arm and fell into a fifty-five gallon drum, which was being used for trash. I immediately started throwing paper out to get to the keys, which had sunk to the bottom. After what seemed like hours, I found them. But then, for some unknown reason, I methodically started putting all the paper back in the trash can. I was scared to death, and my mind insisted that I be neat and tidy! Something just wasn't right with my thought process. Depression had really messed with my mind.

While everyone was still busy yelling and screaming, I scrambled to the door, jumped in the car, and locked the doors immediately. I started the engine as fast as my trembling hands would allow me, and took off. The entire time I feared that he would follow me in his sister's car and try to run me off the road.

Once on the main interstate, I exited and waited in a McDonald's parking lot until I felt the coast was clear. As soon as I arrived in Ohio, I stopped at a payphone to call my parents, and let them know I was all right, and when to expect me. They hadn't thought my idea was a good one and had been fearful for me. After the adrenaline had kicked off and reality settled in, I cried the rest of the way home. I thought to myself, *How could I stay married to someone who I was afraid would hurt me and someone who was mentally abusive?* He was like a ticking time bomb, and I hadn't even told him I wanted a divorce.

Soon the harassing phone calls began. Sometimes he would tell me how much he loved me, and other times he would call to scream obscenities and give me a piece of his mind. He didn't know what he wanted, but he was upset and hurt. The only thing he was sure of was that the boat was his one true love.

The only clothes I had were the ones I had packed to wear at home. The rest of my clothes were still on the boat. He screamed that it was his boat and his belongings. At this point, the only things I wanted off the boat were my silverware and a pair of multi-colored boat shoes I loved. I ended up getting part of my silverware back and that was all.

I lived with my parents for several months while seeking employment. I soon received a lucrative job as a safety coordinator, for a small manufacturing plant in the area. I rented a one-bedroom apartment and moved in with the only furniture I still had left: a day bed and a small black and white television set. My friends graciously gave me dishes, silverware, pots, and pans, and I bought the other necessities. I literally lived in the living room. The bedroom was completely void of furniture. The only reason I had to go in there was to pick out one of the few outfits I had bought to wear. Fortunately, my job with the manufacturing plant afforded me the opportunity to wear jeans most of the time.

It was now on to divorce number three. The pain and the

shame were almost unbearable. I consulted a local attorney, but he was unsure as to how to serve papers to my husband, who, by this time, had returned to Trinidad, and sailed the boat back to St. Thomas in the Virgin Islands. He was now living on the boat and working at a marina. My girlfriend suggested getting on the internet and finding an attorney in St. Thomas to serve him with Ohio divorce papers. I contacted an attorney who explained what would have to happen and he gave me the name of a certified court officer who specialized in serving papers to boaters. I asked him to send me a bill for his time, but he refused. I thought, *God, please bless this man*!

Much to my husband's surprise, he was served papers at his workplace which meant that the divorce would now have to take place in Ohio. He didn't take kindly to this, and I was told he was extremely unpleasant to the gentleman who served him the papers. The divorce was official in December 1996. It was now time to get back to my life.

I prayed, *God, where are you? I need you. My life is a train wreck. I got myself into this situation, but I need you to help me get out*. I knew God heard me, but I wasn't strong enough in my faith to believe he could do anything for me. After all, I had made my own mess, or was it the disease? I wondered, *how can you distinguish the disease from the person?* Now it was up to me to live with it, or forget it and move on with my life.

Job Jumping

"Humble yourselves, therefore, under God's mighty hand, that he may lift you up in due time. Cast all your anxiety on him because he cares for you," (1 Peter 5:6–7 NIV*).*

The job I had taken at the manufacturing plant was not quite as comforting as being home. My job was considered a management position, and it was a union company. I was between a rock and a hard place. On my very first day, I was asked to teach a blood borne pathogens class. I was showing videos and giving my lecture, when one of the employees started to degrade me, the subject, and everything safety stood for. He jumped up from his chair, confronted me face to face, and started to scream obscenities at me. I politely asked him if he wanted to be in the class. He said no. I stated that if he could not behave himself, I didn't want him in the classroom, disturbing the other participants, and I asked him to leave. I continued on and finished the class, extremely upset, but trying not to show it. When I started to go out the door of the training room, six big hefty union officials were waiting for me. They wanted to know what was going to happen to this person. Well, I didn't know. I was naive about union/management relationships and had no idea it was going to be such a big thing. I said that he would probably have to make-up the class in another session. I then went to my boss and explained to her what had happened. At that point, everything broke loose. I felt like I was in way over my head! I hadn't intended for things to get out of control, but evidently management had problems with this person before and was looking for another way to get a mark on record against him. My boss was delighted with me, albeit surprised; I took control of the situation as firmly as I did. It really bothered me that an adult would disrespect me in that way. It made me angry and uncomfortable.

That night I stayed in my closet with the door closed and curled up in a fetal position. I felt safe in the closet, and closed myself in there often. I felt as if the outside walls were crumbling around me, and the closet would protect me. It helped.

About this time I felt the need for something in my life. Since I had sworn off marriage, I decided to adopt a bunny. I was told at the pet store that the bunny was a she, but when I went to have her spayed, I found out differently. His original name was Suzie Q, but that seemed a little inappropriate.

His new name became Chauncey. He was so sweet and fun to watch. His love made me feel whole again.

I soon realized the company was making grave mistakes, and I tried to stick up for what I thought was right. I went strictly by the OSHA Manual and based my decisions on what was legal. Sometimes this made management angry with me, and sometimes it upset the union. This is when my first signs of extreme agitation and aggression started to appear. I wasn't getting any cooperation from the engineering department, and in one of our weekly meetings, I said exactly how I felt about that. A friend of mine at the plant, who was also in a management position, started kicking me under the table, but I ignored him and continued on with my speech. My boss was frozen in her chair, not knowing what to say or do, and the general manager looked shocked, but came up to me later and applauded me for speaking the truth. Nevertheless, I was embarrassed for what I had done and the problems remained unresolved.

I stuck it out until the company announced it was closing down. However, while I was still in the ranks of safety coordinator, and just after they made the announcement, a maintenance man working on a piece of machinery was killed instantly in a freak accident. This devastating event led to my downfall. It wasn't my fault, but I kept asking myself, *what could I have done differently? What if I had yelled a little louder in those meetings and stood my ground?* I had known this was a problem area, but no one had listened to me. I questioned, *why hadn't they listened to me? Why?* This man had a wonderful family, and he was getting ready to retire. Sadness overwhelmed me and my anger mounted. I felt as if my insides had been ripped out. Seeing his lifeless body in the casket at the funeral home added to my sorrow, and I couldn't hold back the tears any longer. I allowed them to flow, I had to. It brought relief. I felt so confused and messed up inside. The pain was gut-wrenching and my feelings were emotionally blurred. The days dragged on and then the engineer called me into his office one day. He began to show me pictures of the maintenance man with his head still in the machine, then a picture after they laid him down. I wanted to vomit, I thought he was being cruel, but then I realized he was just as torn up about the incident as I was. Once enemies, we now became friends in mourning.

Meanwhile, I found a new psychiatrist. I was put on a stronger antidepressant and a stronger anti-anxiety medication to help me cope with the job. It seemed as if I was changing a job, changing a psychiatrist, or changing a husband. All the changes were valid from my point of view and that's what mattered. I really needed a psychiatrist to work with me, because the medication's effectiveness was always short-lived. Some psychiatrists insist a person stay on the medication, even though it isn't working. Their feeling was that it would take three to six months to take effect. However, for me, if the medication didn't work within two months, it wasn't going to work. It didn't seem as if psychiatrists were interested in me as a person. I always felt like a number. I felt that way about medical doctors too. I'm sure they cared. They just have a busy schedule to keep. Psychiatrists handle the *pill* end of it and therapists deal with you if you want to talk. And yes, I've been to several therapists as well who really did a marvelous job, if I would have taken all their advice.

My next job was as a coffee entrepreneur. Pat, the gentleman at the plant who had kicked me under the table, had been downsized, and he was looking into buying a coffee shop. Since I was an avid coffee connoisseur, he asked me to be a sweat equity co-owner. I eagerly accepted the invitation, and off we went into the world of mochas, espressos, and cappuccinos. I became the partner who opened the store in the morning and started making fresh-baked muffins to eat with all the delicious flavored coffees and cappuccinos. It was great, except, I wasn't comfortable dealing with the public. My hands would start to sweat and my heart would palpitate. I was nervous, stressed out, and becoming aggressive to everyone. Pat put up with me because he knew about my depression, but I wasn't happy with the job. I was a quiet person who wanted to work by myself in a corner where no one could see me. Pat was the extrovert and loved the customers. He memorized their names, their drinks, and he made it the successful business that it was.

Meanwhile, I made the decision to go back into secretarial work. I discussed my decision with him and he said he was okay with it, but yet I feel I left Pat hanging, and for that I am ashamed. But the gracious, loving man that he is, never said a word, and we are still close friends today. He continued with the coffee shop for a number of years before he decided to sell it.

Next, it was off to working as a secretary for one of the local fire departments, through an employment agency. The first time I met the fire chief at the interview, my heart started to pitter-patter. It was going to be difficult (but fun) working together with me having feelings for him. It was a wonderful job. Everyone was friendly and easy to get along with. Then, I received a call that I will never forget. The caller wanted to speak to the chief, who was not in the office at the time. The caller informed me that one of our firefighters had been seriously injured (off the job). He was working on a boat when it fell on him, and he had been flown by helicopter to a trauma center in Toledo, Ohio. When the chief returned he asked me to go with him to notify the firefighter's wife. This was heart-wrenching. She didn't feel well and didn't know what to do. We couldn't get her out of the house into the car. I finally ended up helping her change clothes and grabbed her purse. She needed to make one phone call which seemed to take forever and then we kindly forced her into the car. We took her directly to the hospital and a couple of days later her husband died from his injuries. He was given a firefighter's funeral, and the Cathedral was packed. This brought back all the horrible memories of the maintenance man that was killed at the manufacturing plant where I had previously worked.

I immediately went back to my psychiatrist and asked for help. Once again, the medications just didn't seem to be controlling my depression.

Even though the fire department was a party-centered bunch of guys and gals, and I was partying right along with them, I still felt a deep, nagging vacuum, sucking me under the earth's surface. I started making bad decisions and was extremely moody.

I would have fits of aggression; I like to refer to them as "Marla moments," when everyone would cringe. I was always mortified when it was over and would apologize for my behavior, but the "fits" became more and more frequent as time went on. I don't know if I was trying to run away from my fears, my past, my present, or my future.

I had started a personal relationship with an employee at the time and it became difficult because of my position as the administrative assistant. This was difficult because the employee was my boss. In fact, the employee was the chief of the fire department! A personal relationship within a department wasn't a good idea for either of us, especially him. He was one of the nicest men I'd ever met. He was very good looking and had a great laugh. He was also compassionate about my bouts of depression and anxiety, and very loving and caring. He was my prince charming. We had some wonderful times together: eating out, going to movies, and sitting around the house. He could play the guitar and sing, and he loved Eric Clapton music. I could sit and listen to him sing and play for hours.

He and I spent Friday nights going out with the firefighters, having a few drinks, and enjoying ourselves. It was almost too good to be true, but something wasn't quite right. His kids lived in another state, and I knew if he had a chance to go back there, he would do it in a heartbeat. I didn't want to leave my son or my parents again. I also knew I was mentally unstable and didn't want to put anyone through having to live with my critical outbursts. Plus, I was scared to death of making another mistake, and having it end in divorce number four. I would never be able to handle that. It would push me over the edge.

Chauncey, my bunny, didn't like the idea of me being gone so much. He felt neglected. I was at work all day, sometimes I wouldn't get home until late at night, and then I was going out on Friday nights. I'm sure it just didn't seem fair to him. It seemed as if he was trying to tell me something. I loved him so much.

I started to attend church regularly and the Holy Spirit was nudging me to stop sleeping with a man that I hadn't married. I asked him if he would start going to church with me and forego having an intimate relationship, but his response was that he had tried religion and it didn't work for him. He also wanted to continue our intimate relationship. My mind was confused, but we continued to see each other. In order to get out of the fire department, and the precarious position I was in, I got a job at an assisted living facility, working as an administrative secretary. He was very supportive of my move. That meant our relationship could be more open. The job started out as a challenge with programs to set up for printing invoices and getting the place in order, but soon the extra hours started adding up. What was supposed to be an eight hour day, salaried position, soon became a ten hour day and then a twelve hour day. It was extremely stressful, and I had seen, during my past experiences, that stress always worsened my depression. When anything stressed me out, I wanted to go immediately to my safe place, which is home, or in the closet.

Then, quite unexpectedly, my mother, who was only sixty-seven years old, passed away on March 17, 1999. She had become ill with pneumonia and was too weak to handle the trauma. My father and I were at her bedside when she died. Devastation set in! The combination of shock and disbelief made it unbearable. Even though my mother and I hadn't always seen eye-to-eye on everything, she was wonderful, and I loved her very much. Now it was time to help my father adjust to his great loss. The chief stayed with me through it all. He went to the funeral and offered his condolences.

On the day before my mother died, I found out I needed to have a hysterectomy. The surgery took place in April 1999, and only added to the stress in my life. Yes, once again, the chief was by my side before and after the surgery, right along with my dad. My next scare came in March 2000, when my doctor had to do a breast biopsy. I had found a lump the size of a golf ball in my left breast, and thought the worst. However, God was watching over me, and even though I lost part of my left breast, the tumor was benign. My dad was with me on this one, but the chief and I had already decided to go our separate ways. Things would have been different if I knew he wouldn't be heading back to Indiana and he was willing to have a platonic relationship until we were married.

With the death of my mother and two unforeseen surgeries, it became too much to handle a personal relationship. Even though I loved this man very much, the possibility of his moving away still bothered me. In addition, my erratic mood swings made me question my sanity. I didn't know, at the time, that I was bipolar, and this was a symptom of mania. If I had known, and gotten help for it, things may have turned out differently. I thought I had good reasons at the time to break up with him, but once we actually broke up, my life started to disintegrate. Once again I ended up back in the psychiatric ward, with suicidal thoughts. Not only did I feel like a failure, but I also felt numb, empty, worthless, and ashamed. The doctor had assigned a new psychiatrist to me. He talked to me the following morning, and said he felt the medication was working, and he let me go home the same day. Being in the hospital was my cry for help, and no one was listening! I needed someone to talk to and bounce my thoughts off of. I needed someone who could tell me what my thoughts were. I was really mixed up and acting strange. My ex-boyfriend had found a new girlfriend, and I had walked into where she worked that day and started asking some questions. I was jealous he had found someone. One thing led to another, and my ex-boyfriend showed up. Things were said that shouldn't have been said, and now I was in the hospital, needing help to sort everything out and find out why it happened. I instigated the situation, but why? This wasn't the Marla I knew. She would have never done anything like that. There was more wrong with me than severe depression. I needed to get my thoughts on God, and start doing what was right. I hurt so badly from the breakup. It tore my heart to pieces, and I was filled with remorse.

At this point, I started attending church regularly, and took a Foundations 101 class that the church was offering. It was a wonderful class that taught about Jesus Christ as our Savior. At the end of the class, I prayed the prayer of salvation, and accepted the Lord Jesus Christ as my Savior. I truly believed my past transgressions were washed away for good, and I began to start a new life with God. Although I had some setbacks, I knew this was the real thing. A few years later I joined the church and was baptized in the Holy Spirit. Even though I continued to make some bad decisions, I knew that God was with me.

In July 2000, I quit my job at the assisted living facility, to go back to school, and complete my Associate's Degree in Business Management Technology. I thought this would give me a nice break, and take my mind off my hurt; I forgot that I was not as young as I used to be. With the confusion and mind-wandering caused by my severe depression, it was extremely difficult to concentrate, read, listen, and learn. It took absolutely everything out of me to get through the semester, and with two weeks left to go, I just gave up on studying, and decided what will be, will be. I ended up with good grades. God was surely watching over me, and I couldn't have done it without his strength. I graduated in December 2000, from Bowling Green State University, with an Associate of Applied Business Degree in Business Management Technology, with honors. My son, dad, brother, and nephew were there to cheer me on, and for this I was extremely grateful.

Then I began to think, *Now where am I going to get a job?* I wasn't quite sure what my degree was good for, and didn't know where to begin. But, an opportunity soon presented itself. A good friend of mine worked in a legal office, and we were at a restaurant one night when one of the attorneys from the office came in. I knew him well from the coffee shop. She told him I was looking for a job, and he asked me to come interview the next day. I did, and he immediately offered me a job working on sudden acceleration cases, and giving him a hand with a project he was just beginning in Russia. It paid the same as the assisted living facility, but I didn't have health insurance coverage. In essence, I conquered getting my degree, and then went backwards. At least I had an income, and I could bargain for insurance later. I felt I was fortunate to get a job with my history of job-hopping. I had five jobs in a very short period of time, and I had quit each one in one of my darkest moments.

The Mask

"In this world you will have trouble. But take heart! I have overcome the world," (John 16:33, NIV*).*

I once again put on my mask, and ventured out into the world. My new job started out assisting my boss with his plans to renovate a maternity hospital in the Oblast of Balashikha, in Russia. This consisted of working with dignitaries in Russia, including the Minister of Health of Moscow and the Governor of the Oblast of Balashikha, as well as an American architect, and the head of a large pediatric unit in Ohio.

On my first trip to Russia, I was a little apprehensive. The nerves started to kick in, the heart palpitations began, and the depression hung around for good measure. By this time, I was on three different medications, and barely making it. Regrettably, my medications didn't mix well with Russian traditions. The first mountain I had to cross was during our first meeting, when the secretary came in at 10:30 a.m., delivering shots of vodka, biscuits, and chocolate candy. This was their traditional morning break, and it began with consuming a shot of straight vodka. I tried to explain to them that I couldn't drink with my medications, but my boss stated, "While in Russia, do as the Russians do." He then whispered to me, "Don't insult them; drink it." Well, down with the first shot of vodka for the day.

My only participation in the meetings was to take notes and document as much as possible. Basically, we went from one meeting to another with our Russian counterpart yelling at his driver all the way. Thankfully, we had an interpreter who spoke excellent English and Russian, and helped us to decipher the rhetoric. The meetings dragged on until late in the afternoon, and then we would go to the five-star Hotel National in Moscow, where we were staying, to change clothes and freshen up. The hotel was beautiful, yet subdued. The halls were long and narrow with old-fashioned chandeliers that gave off minimal light. The hotel room was unique. There was a faded blue curtain outside the door to the room with a tiny alcove before you got to the door itself. Inside was a twin bed, an armoire, a desk, a luggage holder, and locked bar with a small television on top. The only American channel available was CNN. The bathroom was small, but adequate; however, I couldn't find where to flush the toilet. I looked everywhere, and pushed every button I could find. I would have been embarrassed to call the front desk to ask how to flush it. I finally spotted a white panel that blended into the sparkling white tiles on the wall. I pushed it ever so gently, and the toilet slowly began to flush.

Next it was on to dinner at the posh Pushkin Café. The restaurant proved that great service and delicious food could be found in Russia, if you could afford it. Dinner, once again, included numerous shots of vodka. They served their vodka ice cold, and if you turned your back for an instant, they refilled your shot glass. By this time, I was actually beginning to like vodka, and consumed a little too much. Together with my medications, I felt as if my feet were not touching the floor. It was a very strange sensation–almost like floating out of my closet. But, the only thing the vodka did for me was to make me wobbly, send me deeper into despair, and add to my already multiplying migraine headaches.

When the meetings were over, and I was able to do a little shopping and sight seeing, it came as a welcomed relief. The multi-colored domes were glorious, especially at night, when lit up. I purchased many hand-painted, Russian nesting dolls and even bought some of my favorite vodka. The next thing I knew, we were heading back home again. We left Russia, and had a non-stop flight to LaGuardia airport in New York. There we had to pick up our luggage, go through customs, and catch a puddle-jumper back to Cleveland. We flew into LaGuardia with only a short period of time to catch our connecting flight, but my boss stopped to talk to some people, and left it up to me to get the luggage. I will never forget struggling to pull our luggage off the rounder, and trying to get out of the way of the mobs of people around me. It was too heavy for me to carry the suitcases, plus my purse, and carry-on, so, I ended up crawling on the floor on my hands and knees, pushing the luggage ahead of me. I was totally humiliated! I was also hurt, angry, nervous, depressed, and just plain miserable. Then, as if this wasn't enough, they had to hold the connecting flight on the runway for us, so my boss could go to the bathroom. I sat behind my boss on the plane ride home, and cried all the way. This was a disastrous ending to the trip.

On my second trip to Russia, we were accompanied by an architect and his wife, the head of pediatrics and his wife, my boss's wife, and a photography crew from Notre Dame. Again, the meetings included vodka, and dinner always started with vodka. I had to put on the most durable "smiley face" mask I could find, because my heart and soul felt like it was being crushed beneath a front-end loader. A few of the people in our party would ask, "Marla, are you feeling all right?" I would always answer, "Oh, I'm just tired." Inside, however, I felt empty and isolated. Worse than that, the next day we had a conference scheduled with a list of people that read like the "Who's Who" of Russia.

I expected an office meeting like we had always had in

the past, and was ready with my stenographer's notebook in hand. Much to my surprise the "meeting" was anything but. As we arrived at the meeting place, there were approximately thirty people standing outside, with what looked like luggage bags all around. I thought to myself, *what were they going to do, deport us for trying to help?* I didn't realize, until I stepped out of the car, that they weren't luggage bags, but rather camera bags. The blazing camera bulbs started going off continuously—I could barely keep my eyes open. They were obviously scheduled by the Russians to come and report on our meeting. Thankfully no one asked us any questions. They were just there to cover this news story. Next came a television camera crew, and suddenly a huge, furry, old-fashioned hand muff came down in front of me. I jumped! It was a speaker system to pick up our voices. I could have said a thing or two about that time, but knew I had to keep my mouth shut. I felt like Princess Diana with the rapacious Paparazzi! I just wanted to be left alone.

We entered a large conference room with lengthy, built-in, hard wood tables on both sides of the room, facing each other. There was about a fifteen foot expanse between them. Not exactly what I would call cozy. Huge windows were covered with sheer curtains, and adorned with beautiful, variegated, brown drapes. Parts of the walls were covered with hardwood panels, and the remaining walls were painted delicate, light beige. The room was magnificent! There were seven dignitaries on the Russian side of the room, and seven ordinary people on the American side of the room, plus our interpreter. I don't remember how long the meeting lasted. All that I recall is the relief I felt as I climbed back into the car, and shrank down into the backseat. I thought, *this isn't me.* I was just a small town girl who had wandered into unfamiliar territory. I wanted to go home. I wanted to hide in my house for the rest of my life!

This trip took its toll on me, and I vowed never to return to Russia. The heavy, deep feeling of depression, and the anguish I felt being on public display was unbearable, and I wanted to go home and hide in my closet. I wanted solitude!

My next project was acting as a paralegal during a trial, which I was not. It was a sudden acceleration case in San Antonio, Texas, in which a driver was killed in a car accident. The exhibits were ready to go, and were being shipped to the co-counsel in the case. My stomach churned as I received a quick lesson in what a paralegal does in court, but deep inside I was excited to be seeing our justice system at work. Unfortunately, we failed miserably, and the entire case fell apart. The exhibits quickly got out of order and were strewn about on the prosecutor's table.

The short recesses didn't allow me enough time to get them back in order. We had more than seventy-five pictures of the car, that were to be used in the case, but the office staff had listed them all as one exhibit. The co-counsel in the case was shuffling through all of them in order to find the one he wanted. It was extremely time-consuming and embarrassing. He was upset; the court was mad, and the defendant's attorneys fought to keep from laughing out loud. Heck, there were parts of the trial when I was trying not to laugh. Our case went downhill from there, and we ended up losing it after a brief fifteen-minute deliberation of the jury.

While I was working on the three-week trial, taking notes through lunch and dinner, and typing well into the night, I was afforded the opportunity of staying at a luxurious, five-star hotel, that overlooked the River Walk in San Antonio. I sat on the balcony at night, and soaked in the peaceful silence and solitude. That was my only relief from the heavy depression that had set in during the trial. Working with the family of the deceased created a profound feeling of hopelessness. I was on the eighth floor and standing on the balcony outside looking down at the concrete below. My mind told me to jump, but my heart cried out to God for help, and once again he delivered me. I loved him for helping me get through the terrible times I was going through. These were times when even your parents can't help you out; you just have to believe in God.

The next trip planned was to San Francisco, to meet with an attorney interested in sudden acceleration cases. I flew there with a female attorney from the office to watch how she handled sharing information. I actually knew enough myself to be able to contribute to the conversation. We had a lot of free time, and had some fun driving the coast, and visiting a mutual friend in Pasadena. When it was time to go, the attorney flew home, and I flew back to San Antonio. I spent a couple of days getting the exhibits boxed up and shipped back to Ohio. This having been done, I was more than ready to go home and relax.

My United Airlines flight was scheduled to leave at 7:00 a.m. the next morning, which meant that I needed to be at the airport no later than 5:30 a.m. When I arrived at the ticketing counter, the attendant informed me the flight was cancelled due to maintenance problems with the airplane in New Jersey. "Oh, no," I stammered. She was quickly able to get me on an American Airlines flight that departed San Antonio at 7:15 a.m., with a lay-over in Dallas, then on to Cleveland, Ohio. No problem. My American Airlines flight left promptly at 7:15 a.m. on September 11, 2001.

September 11, 2001

"For I am the Lord, Your God, who takes hold of your right hand and says to you, Do not fear; I will help you," (Isaiah 41:13, NIV*).*

The plane ride was uneventful until we landed in Dallas. When I got off the plane, I noticed a large group of people standing in and around a small bar with their eyes glued to a television set. I thought it was strange, so I went over to see what was happening. Someone in the crowd said, "A plane crashed into the World Trade Center." I glanced at the TV and thought; *the firefighters will put it out.* It didn't dawn on me that it was a commercial airliner that had been deliberately flown into the building. I thought it was a small two-seater plane that had mistakenly gotten too close to the building. I then thought, *Oh dear, I hope no one in the building was hurt.*

I scurried on to find out what gate my connecting flight was leaving from. I could watch television from that gate and be ready to go. I thought, *that's unusual.* The monitor showed my connecting flight leaving from the same gate I came in on. I'd never been that lucky before. Since my flight wasn't scheduled to depart for a couple of hours, I decided to join the growing crowd around the television set. I arrived just as the announcer was screaming, "Oh no, no, this can't be happening!" As they showed video of a second plane crashing into the second tower, my heart dropped to my toes. When someone said it was an American Airlines flight, I began to panic. It was like a bad dream that you want to wake up from, but your eyes won't open. Then as word slowly crept out that the Pentagon was also hit, my heart started pounding. I thought, *Oh dear Lord, We're under attack!* Shortly thereafter, a woman's voice penetrated the airport. She announced over the loudspeaker that all American Airline flights had been cancelled. I quickly ran to the ticket counter to try to get a different flight out, because I wanted to be home with all this happening. I was scared!

I stopped at a payphone to call my father, and let him know what was happening, and that I was okay. But, while we were still talking, the loudspeaker again crackled to attention, and the airport director announced the airport was closed. I quickly put down the payphone and ran to the hotel phones to get a room for the night. Thankfully, I beat the crowd and was able to get a hotel room close to the airport. The problem was getting out of the airport. *Read the signs, Marla, you want the shuttle services to local hotels.* If the United States was being attacked, I certainly didn't want to be at the Dallas airport. As I started walking down the hall to find the exit for hotel buses, a lady stopped in front of me and asked if I was stranded. I told her yes, but I had a hotel room. She told me that if it fell through, to give her a call on her cell phone. She offered to pick me up, and said I could stay with her and her husband who lived in Dallas. She then wrote down her cell phone number on a scrap piece of paper, and handed it to me. I was so grateful and shocked that a complete stranger would take me into her home. I thanked her, and she asked if I would like to pray with her. I quickly agreed, and the hustle and bustle surrounding us suddenly stopped. We prayed together for the lives of all the people in the planes and buildings. This was my wake-up call. I needed God in my life permanently. I needed to know him, have a personal relationship with him, trust him, and obey him. I was working on it, but I needed to work harder.

Life changed for me that day, as it did for so many people. Suddenly, God was important. All the things I learned in Sunday school came back to me: how faithful, caring, and loving he was. The destruction of our nation's symbols of security came to me as shock, fear, disbelief, and anger. My mood grew somber as I struggled to get my luggage. However, my luggage didn't come. It had been impounded by security. I thought, *that was okay, I have a clean pair of socks and underwear in my carry-on case.*

When I arrived at the hotel, people were shouting and demanding rooms without having a reservation. Their anger came from fear. As I stood in my hotel room, looking out my window that faced the airport, I felt numb. My heart cried out to everyone on the planes and in the towers, but the tears wouldn't flow. I was petrified and frozen with horror on one side and wishing I had been on one of the planes that crashed on the other side. I would have willingly gone in someone else's place in order to give them life. My thoughts plunged me deeper into depression as I thought about suicide. I forced myself to call my father, and let him know I was all right and where I was staying. I then called the office, where everyone was very relieved I was safe. My boss was stranded in Washington, D.C. His hotel was under lock-down, and from the roof of the hotel he could see the smoke from the Pentagon.

There were so many questions going through my head. *How could this happen? What was wrong with the world? Was this the end? Who did this? Why did they do it?* There were so many questions, yet so few answers. My mind churned like water in a washing machine. This was the first time I could ever remember wanting to be with people, and not be alone. I went down to the bar to get a drink and a bite to eat, and watch the large screen TV. All of a sudden, it was as if I had known everyone for years. People were talking, commenting, expressing anger, and crying: we all clung together. We hugged, comforted each other, and intently listened to CNN. I lost a solid gold leaf earring at the bar. Somehow, I spotted it, and was thankful no one had taken it.

My mind wondered for a moment and I had to think, *where am I? Oh yes, Dallas.* My mind became jumbled, and I couldn't think rationally. It wasn't just the circumstances around me that was causing my disorientation, but rather the deep depression and anxiety taking hold. I needed something to cushion my mind, and protect it from itself. The medications weren't working, as usual. Well, I guess they were working to keep me from committing suicide. But still, *maybe another drink would help.* The people around me suddenly became insignificant. I rode from emotion to emotion in a way that was somewhat absurd. Confusion doesn't describe it. It's far more than that. It seems almost as if I was unplugged from the rest of the world, and the voices sounded as if they were coming from a tunnel. I needed to get back to my room before someone noticed I was going mad! Now, where did I put that earring?

> Wednesday, September 12, 2001—Headlines
> *The Dallas Morning News*–"War at home"
> *The Advocate (Newark, Ohio)*–"American Nightmare"
> *The Indianapolis Star*–"Day of Death"

The next day, The Dallas Morning News headline read "War at Home." This was America, and we were attacked on American soil. Yes, this was "War at Home." The horror of September 11, 2001, will stay with me forever, as it will so many. I prayed to God that he would help the victims and relatives of all the people who had died. It seemed impossible that God could be with so many people at one time, but with God all things are possible. I decided that I was not going to live in bondage anymore. I can't do anything about my past, but I could do something about my future. I needed to start changing how my environment affected my depression so that I could start enjoying my life. We never know when the time will come that Jesus will return.

My head was slightly clearer the next day, but the airport was still closed. It looked like I would be washing my clothes. Fortunately, I had thrown my bathing suit into my carry-on case while I was hurriedly packing in San Antonio. I put it on, and washed all my clothes together, to save on the cost of detergent in the hotel Laundromat. Whites, darks, and lights all together, it didn't make a difference at this point in time. I was in a fog and nothing made sense anyway.

On Thursday, I took the hotel shuttle to the airport. I found that there would be some flights departing that evening. My flight was scheduled to leave early in the evening. I went back to the hotel, put on my bathing suit, got a drink from the bar, and went out to sit by the pool. The sky was a beautiful dark blue and the sun was shining brightly. Nevertheless, it felt eerie with no planes in the sky.

No white streams of puffy pillows from jet engines slowly dissipating into thin air.

Finally it was time to go to the airport and board my American Airlines flight. I was going from Dallas to Cleveland. I scurried to pack and made it to the airport and through security rather quickly. Once inside, the concourse was empty, eating places were closed, and terminals stood deserted. There were only a few passengers, but plenty of police, security agents, FBI agents, and National Guard units. When my flight departed, the plane was less than one-quarter full, and the back half was dark. They had seated everyone in the front of the plane. The flight was uneventful. Even though I felt safe and secure, I prayed that the flight would land safely.

When I arrived at Cleveland Hopkins Airport, it was close to midnight, and no one was around, including security. I retrieved my suitcase, walked through the dimly lit concourse, and out to the parking garage alone.

I was unable to sleep very well, so I ended up going to work at my regularly scheduled time the next day. My boss was already back. He had rented a limousine to drive him from Washington, D.C. back to Ohio. It was then that he told me the plan for another trip to Russia in November. I can remember thinking, after what just happened, *you're out of your mind.* But I respectfully kept my mouth shut. I would only have a couple of days to think about this because the process would soon begin to get a visa. The next day I went into my boss's office and explained to him why I wouldn't be going to Russia. I cried through the entire explanation. My depression was rearing its ugly head. He asked me what was wrong, but I fluffed it off as just being tired. He was disappointed that I wouldn't be going to Russia with him because he had just appointed me project manager, but evidently he decided not to say anything. Within two weeks I had obtained another job and gave him my two-week notice. I had worked for him less than a year. As it happened, he no longer required an *extra hand* on his trips to Russia so he wasn't really that upset. I was feeling free because I already had another job and was looking forward to it. Everything worked out for the best.

Breakdown

"He will cover you with his feathers, and under his wings you will find refuge; his faithfulness will be your shield and rampart," (Psalm 91:4, NIV*).*

Here was one more new job, this time as an executive assistant. With it came a very nice raise in pay, but it also came with more responsibility and longer hours. The place was a mess when I started and looked as if it hadn't been cleaned for years. I wore white wool slacks and a light blue wool blazer to work on my first day and was afraid to sit down because the chair was so filthy. I went to open the closet door to hang up my coat and stuff started falling out. When I finally opened it enough to get a good look, I saw piles and piles of paperwork stacked waist high. I thought, *Oh dear, this doesn't look good.* To top off my first day at work, I was also suffering from horrible withdrawal symptoms from Xanax. I had decided to start getting off my medication on my own and started with Xanax, an anti-anxiety medication.

My entire body was trembling inside and I could barely keep it together outside. My mind was like a whirlwind and my stomach rolled. When I left for lunch, I was shaking so badly that I had trouble getting the car keys in the ignition. It never dawned on me that it was the sudden and complete withdrawal from the Xanax. I hesitated to go back to work after lunch. I felt horrible and wasn't pleased with the mess I saw. Nevertheless, I like to organize, so I timidly returned to work. The trembling went on for days before my mind was eased. My girlfriend said that she read on the internet that you were never supposed to go "cold turkey" off a tranquilizer. I looked up Xanax immediately and the warnings on the page glared at me. I instantly popped a Xanax into my mouth and swallowed it, praying that it would ease the trembling. It worked! My trembling stopped, my stomach returned to normal, and the inside of me felt peaceful for the first time in days. I can't describe the relief I felt, it was so overwhelming. The article said to go off Xanax one-half pill at a time in two week increments. Okay, it looked like I would have to go off of my medications more slowly. I didn't really understand why I was trying to get off my medication in the first place. Taking pills every morning and every night was complicated and tiresome, but it didn't bother me that much. I wanted to prove to myself that I didn't need them anymore. However, it was evident that I needed the medication. I was unbalanced and spiraling into yet another deep depression. I was apathetic and sad. The weight loss, fatigue, physical illness, self-imposed isolation, and total exhaustion forced me back on my medications.

I worked as an executive assistant for this employer, and my main job was to assist a board of directors. I spent hours of my time typing minutes for the board and just about every committee meeting they had. During special events, I would work until the wee hours of the following morning, just to keep up with the workload. At this point in time, I joined the smoking crowd for the temporary relief nicotine gave to me. It seemed to help calm me down, or was it my imagination? This was the worst thing I could have done, especially knowing the dangers of cigarette smoking, or was I really concerned about the dangers?

After about two years, I started turning sour. I starting hating the job for no reason and I become despondent, agitated, aggressive, and unkind to everyone, even while on medications. Word started getting around. At about the same time, I was burdened with a new boss who refused to admit I was his assistant. He typed his own letters, opened his own mail, and gave his daily itinerary to another employee. I felt totally out of the loop. It really hurt my feelings that I wasn't being acknowledged. They say the opposite of love is not hate, but indifference. How true that is! My body felt like smoke escaping through the bottom of a door. No one seemed to notice, and yet again, everyone seemed to notice. I became very self-conscious. I also became more miserable and found myself making the people around me just as miserable. I would yell, scream, and once even flung my dictionary across the room, almost breaking a window. I felt psychotic! It had to stop, but I couldn't control it. *What was happening to me?* This was not me, and this was not depression.

I'd go home each night and think about hooking up a hose to the exhaust system of my car and placing the hose in the car window with the garage door closed. It was winter, my neighbors had gone to Arizona, and no one would hear the car running. It seemed like such a simple thing to do, and such a peaceful way to leave this messed-up world. The pain was excruciating. My heart physically ached. *What was happening? It didn't use to be like this.* I liked my job at one point. I didn't want to live like this anymore. I didn't know what was happening to me. But, nevertheless, I would go back to work each day and would continue to lose control.

When I explained to my psychiatrist what was happening, she started asking me questions about my spending. I thought, *what do my spending habits have to do with my psychotic outbursts?* She continued to ask, but I just couldn't form the words on my lips. *Are you supposed to tell your psychiatrist everything*? It was difficult to talk about money. *How could I tell her that I had gone on a shopping spree and bought a $900 pant suit and a $200 plain black skirt? Or that I was on a high one day and bought a $1,000 Thomas Kincaid painting? How could I tell her about the* *time I was feeling unusually high and suddenly decided to buy a $22,000 Jeep, which I only kept for six months? Then there was the time I bought a $500 diamond ring I had no use for and a $100 stuffed giraffe.*

There were times that I would feel so happy and carefree that I started talking a mile a minute, and I was unable to shut up. I had moments of total exhilaration over nothing. *How could I describe to her how extremely aggressive and agitated I was? No, I couldn't tell her those things because I was sweet, kind, gentle, level-headed, introverted Marla.* To tell her about these types of episodes would be admitting that there was more to my disease than just depression.

Finally, one day in her office, she asked me if I had a Bible and believed in God. I broke into tears as I told her I had a Bible, believed in God, and I was going to church. God put it on my heart to tell her everything at that moment. As I started blurting out about the spending sprees and the aggressive behavior, she realized I was not being treated for the proper disease. After much questioning and further sessions, in June 2004, she diagnosed me with bipolar disorder, and I began a series of new medications. My doctor listed a number of symptoms of bipolar disorder: aggressive mood, high energy level, poor judgment, spending sprees, impulsive sexual indiscretion, alcohol and drug abuse, just to name a few. I also found out that if one is medicated strictly for depression and not for bipolar disorder, the bipolar disorder becomes more pronounced. However, the bipolar medications were inadequate, and the bipolar disorder became pronounced for me. In June 2005, I quit my lucrative job because I was so infuriated with life. I actually feared that I would hurt someone other than myself. I didn't have another job, and I didn't care! My thought process wasn't operating. I felt as if I had lost my sanity. Even though I had given a two-week notice, they asked me to leave the same day. That was the end for me. I had never been so humiliated in my life.

My psychiatrist referred me to someone else because she was unable to help me. She told me that the new psychiatrist was more familiar with mixing different medications and gaining favorable results. I was now on my tenth psychiatrist and I had gone through three licensed, professional psychologists as well. My new psychiatrist confirmed the diagnosis of bipolar disorder and, by the end of 2005, I was on four different medications. By the time we were well into 2006, the medications increased to five, then six. By this time, I was taking 120 mg of Cymbalta, 300 mg of Lithium, 1.5 mg of Klonopin, 50 mg of Trazodone, 5 mg of Abilify, and 200 mg of Lamictal each day. The spending sprees had become less frequent, the outbursts of aggression subsided, but the depression was still debilitating. The thing that scared me the most was that I was still not working. I didn't know if the spending sprees and outbursts of aggression would come back if I added the stress of a full-time job. Even though I was avidly sending out applications and answering practically every advertisement in the newspaper, it didn't seem as if I was getting many calls for interviews. I sent out fifty resumes, had five interviews, and three job offers. I eagerly accepted the job offers and then would quit after one day. I wanted to be home alone; I wanted silence and solitude. I couldn't stand to be out of the house.

Maybe it was because of my active pursuit of employment and my concern of working again, along with the bad memories, but I was suddenly thrown into another manic attack. I signed up for classes at a Christian university in order to get a psychology degree. I was so eager to get back into college and turn my life around. I was in a manic stage. I wanted to learn more about my depression and bipolar disorder. I wanted to know what made me the way I was when I wasn't on the right combination of pills. I wanted to know more about the disease and why there was a stigma attached to it. But my mind moved so fast.

The next day I contacted the university to change my degree to an Associate degree in Religion. Fantastic, learn the Bible, get to know the Word better, and become more intimate with God. I signed up for two summer classes. I wanted knowledge and intimacy. I thought this would be my perfect opportunity. I was in Bible studies at church, but I wanted more. I was also fearful of going back to work and the possibility of getting back into a situation like I had been in. I didn't want to fight anymore, I didn't want to be frustrated anymore, I didn't want to yell and scream anymore, I wanted my life back, and I saw this as one way to do it. I just wanted peace, and I needed God in my life for that. I had to have it, my brain craved it. I don't think I was feeling at the moment, I was just caught up in the fast-paced world of manic-depression! I was desperate for peace, and until the right pill combination made me better, I had to create a way to bring myself peace—although it's God that brings you peace. I was ecstatic and ordered my books immediately. Then came the down side of mania. Within two days after receiving my books, I changed my mind. I cancelled the classes, sent back the books, and gave up on the idea. I was totally irrational to say the least.

I wanted to get off some of my medications. I wanted to be able to concentrate more, remember things, make decisions, and stick to them. I felt like I was in a medication fog. I felt like I was going crazy and told my psychiatrist what I had done. Months later, when I was more stable, she asked, "No more signing up for seminary?" I replied, "Not at the moment." Humor always helps!

After attempting to get social security disability and being denied, I finally accepted a job at a local department store working part-time in the stockroom during the holiday season. I had gone from making more than $33,000 a year to making $6.50 an hour filling rolling racks with clothing and opening boxes for the floor associates. Even as a stock associate, I wanted to be perfect in everything I did, and I worked extremely hard for that $6.50 per hour, but I enjoyed it and there was no pressure.

By this time, 2005 had come and gone, and 2006 wasn't looking the best. My seasonal job ended the first week of

February, and the intense depression started coming in waves. I was out to sea, under water, and struggling to breathe one week, and then the next week I would be lapping at a sandy shore, basking in the sunlight, only to go rolling back out to sea again the following week. I could no longer take the depression. I would sleep most of the day and all night. I couldn't concentrate, and I couldn't get anything accomplished. It took me a month to clean my house, and then I'd have to start all over again. My energy level was nil, and thoughts of suicide were constantly in my mind.

During this time I was trying everything to get help. My doctor suggested ECT (electroconvulsive therapy). I decided to look into it and made an appointment at a major clinic. The psychiatrist there advised me that I would probably have to have a treatment every other day for three weeks. Then he told me that I would probably be on maintenance treatments at least once a month for the rest of my life. In other words, the initial treatment wouldn't last and successive treatments would become less and less effective. With the memory loss involved, and the idea of getting shocked to the point of causing a seizure, my hopes for this procedure were dwindling. This treatment wasn't for me! Let me make it perfectly clear that this is not to say that ECT is not for anyone. It has worked and made the difference in millions of people's lives. It just wasn't for me.

One day my father saw an article in a newspaper about VNS (Vagus nerve stimulation) Therapy for severe, recurrent, treatment-resistant depression. I asked my doctor about it and she said she had read about it in a psychiatric article, and it would be an option. I ended up sending for more information. At first I thought it was too invasive, and then I realized, *what have I got to lose?*

VNS Therapy requires the implantation of a pulse generator (similar to a pacemaker) inside the left chest, along with a flexible wire that is connected to the left Vagus nerve, through an incision in one of the folds of the neck. The pulse generator and thin, flexible wire deliver mild pulses to the left Vagus nerve. The Vagus nerve delivers the pulses from the generator to the areas of the brain that are involved in the regulation of mood. Beyond the operation itself it is typically painless because the Vagus nerve does not contain pain fibers. VNS Therapy stimulation is regular, automatic, is on twenty-four hours a day, and is normally unnoticeable. My device was manufactured by Cyberonics © which has an excellent Nurse Case Manager program to walk you through all the obstacles. (Refer to "For More Information" in the Appendix)

After surgery, I waited two weeks to heal and then the device was turned on in my psychiatrist's office. A two-inch thick wand-like device (like a hand-held mirror) was held over the stimulator while programming is done on a hand-held computer. When I was ready, the psychiatrist activated the device. It was first activated to .25 milliamps, and then increased in increments of .25 milliamps every two weeks until I reached 1.00 milliamp. Then I waited for a period of time, usually one to two months. If necessary, the device could be taken to 1.25 milliamps.

I continued to go to church and prayed for God's direction. I also continued to tithe like the Bible says to, even though I didn't have a job. I was optimistic about the VNS Therapy procedure; I loved God and prayed for his will to be done, not mine.

New Hope

"For in this hope we were saved. But hope that is seen is no hope at all. Who hopes for what he already has? But if we hope for what we do not yet have, we wait for it patiently," (Romans 8:24–25, NIV*).*

I had suffered thirty-six years with a disease that I was trying to get a grip on. It just didn't seem fair that my insurance company didn't want me to get well again. After all, if I got well and off some medications, it might save them money in the long run. The bureaucracy was so much to handle. No one would commit themselves to answering any of my questions. My insurance company was willing to pay thousands of dollars for hundreds of ECT treatments, but did not want to pay for the VNS Therapy that had been approved by the FDA. I was still paying big bucks for my insurance and was running out of money without a full-time job. Fighting an insurance company is like fighting "big brother." I tried, unsuccessfully, for more than a year to get them to pay for the surgery and implant. It was a very well known insurance company, but I ended up going through four appeal processes and then a final external review. All the answers were "no," and by now my insurance had expired. I had worked hard to try to get the insurance company to pay. I wrote a dozen letters to both the insurance company and the Ohio Department of Insurance, to no avail. I realized I had depleted my time and energy without calling on God. God can cure the soul, but there are times when he wants you to go through the trial so you will lean on him. The situation looked bleak. *What should I do? Here I was, fifty-one years old, no job, no insurance and in desperate need of an operation that could possibly save my life!*

Then I found out that the company that manufactures the VNS device, Cyberonics ©, had an Access program developed for individuals in my situation. There were strict qualifications regarding chronic, recurrent, and treatment-resistant depression, along with not having the ability to pay for the surgery and not having insurance. In addition, a person had to find a doctor that was willing to do the operation free of charge and a hospital that was willing to donate its out-patient surgery room and instruments. The company would then donate the VNS device if a person qualified under their program. Believe it or not, I found a doctor and hospital that agreed to do the surgery. I filled out the required forms and turned it all over to God. If his way to help me was through VNS Therapy, then everything would come together. If not, then God had a different plan to heal me. VNS Therapy would work if it was in God's plan for my life.

I was still on six medications that I could not afford to pay for. It was humiliating for me to get prescription assistance, but I needed it. There were forms to fill out, pay stubs to attach, and verification that I did not have insurance, but it was all worth it because of the high costs of some of my medications. I never want to go through this process again in my lifetime.

Meanwhile, through all the insurance appeals, doctor visits, pain, and misery, I was trying to quit smoking. I wondered to myself, *why is it so difficult?* I had only been smoking for about four years. I should have been able to quit in a week or two, or so I thought. I had developed an addiction to cigarettes. They had become a valuable coping device for me. I felt that I needed them to get me through the day. It was probably all in my head, but they seemed to give me a little burst of energy to get my household cleaning chores done. They also seemed to help me calm down when I was irritable; they helped me to relax, and they gave me something to do when I was bored or needed a break. A cigarette was like a floating buoy in a vast ocean of water. It was something for me to hold on to until help arrived.

I could tell I had become addicted because I refused to

smoke in the house (I didn't like the smell of smoke getting into the furniture), so I would smoke in the garage. I had a small table and chair set up where I would sit and sip my coffee and smoke my cigarettes. I realized that if I really wanted to quit, I needed to take away my creature comforts, so I sold the table and chairs in a garage sale. Then I would sit on a thick woven rug that I had on the floor. When that didn't work, I threw out the rug. Well, if you know Ohio weather, winter can get mighty cold. I would put on my winter coat, wrap myself in a blanket, and sit on the cold garage floor—just for a cigarette.

When I got up to thirteen to fourteen cigarettes a day, I knew I had to do something. I tried everything from the patch, to nasal spray, to nicotine inhalers, to going cold turkey, and I just couldn't stop. I then set out to decrease my intake and finally worked my way down to five to eight cigarettes per day. Again, I thought, *it should be easy to quit now.* No such luck. I can't tell you how many packs of cigarettes I flushed down the toilet or broke up and threw in the trash with hopes of quitting. Just when I thought I could do it, I would go through the trash to pull out cigarette butts that still had enough cigarette left to burn, and smoke them. Even the thought of it disgusted me, but I was really hooked! I felt it was imperative to get off cigarettes, and I felt that God wanted me to quit and needed me to be obedient. I knew what was right, but before long I was up to smoking approximately a pack of cigarettes a day.

I was still having decision-making problems. I felt like

I was on a roller-coaster. I had a bunny named Chauncey who lived to be ten years old. He was wonderful. Then in December 2005, Chauncey got sick. After he passed away on December 14, I decided to get a dog. I purchased a puppy from a breeder and took her back two days later because I couldn't handle the adjustment. Two days later I picked her up again because I missed her and then within a week I took her back for good. I just couldn't make decisions.

In January 2006, I decided to get another bunny. Before long came bunny number two. They were both so cute and loveable. I had Pumpkin neutered and Princess spayed and I was really enjoying them. Then, all of a sudden, I made a decision to give them away and sell their cages with them. I don't really know why I decided to sell them, other than I didn't get a chance to let them out of their cages that often, and I felt a family with children would enjoy them more. Maybe someone else could give them more love than I could, instead of just cleaning their cages and changing their food and water. This is another example of my mind going eighty miles an hour down the wrong side of the highway. I felt like I was making major life decisions in a day. Plus, I was following through with them. Deciding to sell the bunnies and having someone buy them took place in less that a span of a week. I soon regretted my decision, but it was too late, and I wasn't going to get any more pets. I just wanted to be by myself and not have to worry about someone or something else. My worry was whether anyone would take both of the bunnies. They couldn't be separated because they had bonded so well, and I knew Pumpkin, my male tan and white Dutch, would die if he was separated from Princess, my female black and white Holland Lop. I put an advertisement in the newspaper on a Friday and they were gone by 4:00 p.m. on Saturday. It was sad to see them go, I loved them so much, but I wasn't able to give them enough attention at this point in my life. I made sure that they were going to a good home where there would be children and where they would be loved and well taken care of. As I sat on my sofa writing this, I looked across the room at a large, white, blank wall where their shiny blue cages used to be, and it made me sad. *No more pets*! I have enough problems taking care of myself. My mixed-up emotions and whirling mind made it impossible to be practical anymore. Nevertheless, in April 2007, I ended up adopting a cat from the Society for the Prevention of Cruelty to Animals. She is a black cat with a white belly and her name is Katie Kaye. I love her dearly and she is a big part of my life now.

Waiting is one of the most difficult things we do, especially when the years go by and we see no fulfillment of our hopes and dreams. All I wanted was relief from my depression and anxiety. I wanted to be able to go back to working full-time without worrying whether or not I would knock somebody's head off or cry myself to sleep every night. I wanted to quit biting my nails and the skin around them. I wanted to stop crumbling, and start building a new future. I wanted to start making decisions and stick to them. I didn't want a high-powered day job. I wanted to make a living wage, have health insurance, and work at a place where I didn't have to be brilliant all the time.

The days ticked by in their twenty-four hour allotted increments as I waited patiently for word on my VNS Therapy. Every day was the same, no messages and no phone calls. I'd pray each day for an answer, but it wouldn't come. I was trying so hard to wait, but nonetheless, my anxiety level continued to rise. I started reading Bible verses every day regarding "waiting" and came upon these which became favorites of mine:

> *"For in this hope we were saved. But hope that is seen is no hope at all. Who hopes for what he already has? But if we hope for what we do not yet have, we wait for it patiently," (Romans* 8:24–25, NIV*).*
>
> *"Now faith is being sure of what we hope for and certain of what we do not see," (Hebrews* 11:1, NIV*).*

I revisited these verses day after day. Waiting, wondering, wishing, hoping, and praying. The depression was squeezing my heart, and I felt immovable as if in a strait jacket. The torment wouldn't go away and the only relief I experienced was when I was asleep. I took two-hour naps every afternoon. I would read a little, write a little, and pray each day. I was taking a Beth Moore Bible study on the book of Daniel and spent about forty-five minutes each day doing the homework. I was trying to do anything worthwhile to keep my mind busy. Tax season was approaching–time to get my medical and prescription bills in order.

On Friday, January 26, 2007, my prayers were answered. What I had attempted to accomplish for more than a year unsuccessfully, God accomplished in three months! God had opened a door for me that I thought was sealed shut. What a miracle! I had been approved for the VNS Access Program. I was able to have the surgery that I hoped would help my depression. What a relief. I was eager to make an appointment for a consultation with my surgeon.

VNS Surgery

"Yet *the Lord longs to be gracious to you; he rises up to show you compassion. For the Lord is a God of justice. Blessed are all who wait for him!*" *(Isaiah* 30:18, NIV*).*

My consultation was scheduled for February 14, 2007. How appropriate, Valentine's Day. As I waited for the day of my VNS consultation appointment to arrive, I started making some decisions in my life. My brother's wife had wanted me to work for her in her web design business, so I decided it was time to take her up on her gracious proposal. I went back to doing what God gave me the gifts and talents to do best. I loved typing and working with the computer and this was my golden opportunity. I would be able to work out of my home. Black Crow Designs was based out of Pennsylvania, so I would be working long distance. Thank goodness the internet makes this possible. This opportunity would allow me to set my own hours and be able to make my doctor appointments whenever necessary. I still wouldn't have insurance coverage, but I hadn't had it at the department store and this would be a little more income and definitely better hours. Plus, there was always the possibility of finding another part-time job with benefits down the road.

Unfortunately, my consultation appointment came and went. Mother Nature decided that Ohio was going to have its first blizzard in more than a decade, and wouldn't you know, it hit the day before my consultation. The surgeon cancelled all his appointments for the following day because it was predicted to become worse overnight. I was extremely frustrated and the nurse at the other end of the phone picked up on it immediately. She apologized and rescheduled my appointment for Tuesday, February 20, 2007. I thanked her and relaxed a little; after all, that was only six days away. Six days felt like ages away. I was so excited about the surgery and couldn't wait to have it done. I'd been waiting for it for so long and now it was finally here.

Finally, consultation day arrived, and I eagerly drove to Toledo to meet the doctor who would be doing my surgery. He was a good-looking man and very kind, but direct. He told me what would be happening and explained the procedure in more depth. He explained that he would be making two incisions, one in the fold of my lower left neck and one vertically in my left chest. The (pacemaker) stimulator would be inserted into my chest in a pocket just under my skin and the connecting wire would be threaded up into my neck with a special tool. The wire would then be connected to my Vagus nerve. I had a list of questions that I wanted to ask and he patiently answered each one of them. The main question was if they would be using stitches or staples to close my surgery wounds. He stated that he would be using absorbable stitches with surgical tape over them. This made me feel more comfortable. I dreaded the thought of staples, but I could handle stitches. However, absorbable stitches with surgical tape were even better. They were unable to give me the surgery date, but said they would call me the next day. Oh no, I had come this far and still no surgery date. This was aggravating, but since I had suffered from depression for thirty-five years, what was another day going to matter.

The following day I received the call I had been waiting for. My surgery was scheduled for Tuesday, March 13, 2007, and my preliminary testing would be done on February 28th. I had to pinch myself to be sure this was actually happening. I felt that God had brought me through depression and was now going to bring me out of it. I said out loud, *Lord, thank you for all the wonderful things you have done in my life.*

Once I was aware of my preliminary testing date and my surgery date, it was now time to drive to Pennsylvania to learn my new job. I left on Thursday so that I would be back in time on Tuesday to make it to my preliminary testing appointment.

My training ended abruptly when a computer hacker attacked the server and most of my sister-in-law's web sites were affected. In addition, my niece was diagnosed with pneumonia and was put in the hospital for the weekend, so we had my two nephews to take care of. Despite all this, I was able to get a small amount of training in, but I would have to learn more after I returned home. The training that I was getting at home was complicated, yet enjoyable. I loved working with the computer again!

My preliminary tests were simple. They used the results from a recent blood test and I had just had an EKG, so all they had to do was a short physical. Now I only had to wait for my surgery date.

Time flew by, and before I knew it the time had come. It was a beautiful day with temperatures in the fifties. My dad and I left in the morning to head for the hospital in Toledo. We parked the car, found the Surgery Center, and waited in a large, comfortable, beautifully decorated waiting area until they called my name. I was taken upstairs to a pre-operative area to get prepped for surgery. It had beds on both sides of the room. It was separated by hanging curtains with a nurses' station in the middle. I changed into one of their flattering hospital gowns, and Nurse Rose promptly started a saline IV with an antibiotic drip. My father was brought up to stay with me until surgery. I had a visit from the anesthesiologist and two of Dr. Kasper's assistants. Everyone was thoughtful and caring.

Before long they were ready to wheel me into surgery. I kissed my dad good-bye and off I went.

The operating room was a sterile white room with silver surgical instruments lying on a table. Bright lights flooded the entire room. I scooted over to the operating table and a mask was placed over my face. I instantly drifted off to sleep.

When I began to regain consciousness, a different nurse stood at the end of my bed by a bed table covered with charts. She kept saying, "Marla, take deep breaths." I would take a few deep breaths and doze off again, only to awaken to the words, "Marla, take deep breaths." This continued until I was awake enough to realize I was out of surgery. My nurse quickly transferred me to a chair to get me breathing normally and then my father was allowed in to see me.

I must have been white as a ghost, because the first thing my dad said was, "It looks like you're going to be staying the night." I drank some water and nibbled on a few graham crackers before getting dressed and being discharged. I was not allowed a prescription painkiller because of my allergy to codeine so they told me to take extra-strength Tylenol. On the way home we went through a McDonald's drive-thru and after eating a sandwich, fries, and drinking a diet Coke, I felt much better. It relieved my dad when he started to see some color in my cheeks again. All was well and we drove home.

A couple of days later when I was able to remove the

bandages and take a shower, I measured my incisions. My neck incision was three inches long and my chest incision was three and one-half inches long. No wonder I wasn't feeling too perky yet. Nonetheless, I was back to work on Friday morning and working on this book during the evening. I didn't have much pain; it was just sore and difficult to move my neck from side to side. I had a tendency to move my entire body. I started doing exercises to get my neck moving a little more each day and before long I was back to half my normal neck movement. The bandages kept me from moving it any further.

It was important for me to remember that nobody just snaps out of a surgery such as this, but I was moving my neck and off Tylenol two days after surgery. Everyone is different, so I didn't get discouraged; I was feeling like myself again in no time.

Activating the VNS Device

"And we know that in all things God works for the good of those who love him and who have been called according to his purpose," (Romans 8:28, NIV*).*

The day had arrived to activate the VNS Therapy unit. I didn't exactly know what to expect because everyone has a different reaction when the device is first turned on. My psychiatrist was at the controls with the Cyberonics© Representative, Carolyn, explaining what to do and my doctor's registered nurse, Debbie, was there to watch the event unfold. They plugged the information into the hand-held computer as I held the wand over my stimulator and asked me if I was ready. I'd been ready for this day for more than a year and told them to go ahead. I didn't feel a thing. My mind was racing. What if the stimulator was defective or what if the hand-held computer wasn't working? Would they have to do the surgery all over again?

They asked how I felt and I said, "I don't know, turn it on."

"It's on," my doctor said.

"Are you sure you turned it on?" I asked. They all laughed and assured me it had been activated. I hadn't felt a thing, not even the urge to cough. I thought, *it can't really be turned on or I would feel something. Just as I was about to express my worry over the situation, I felt a mild impulse in my neck and realized it was working. Wow, this is easy.* They had turned it on to the first setting which was .25 milliamps. In two weeks they would take me up to .50 milliamps. I was eager for my next appointment and I spent the time working at my part-time job and celebrating Easter at my brother's house. All his children and grandchildren visited, along with their dogs. At one point there were five grandchildren in the house, five big dogs, and a poor little cat named Pumpkin who stayed in the bedroom. The kids were excited about their Easter baskets and I was excited remembering that Christ had risen to glory. We had a tremendous time and the days passed quickly.

It was now time for step two. My stimulator would be ramped up to .50 milliamps. My doctor, once again, was at the controls while Carolyn watched over her. My dad also wanted to see how the procedure was done so I invited him in as well. This time was different. The second it was activated to a higher level, I was aware of a pounding sensation on the left side of my neck. It caused me to cough briefly and the sensation surprised me. There was no doubt in my mind that the stimulator was working.

I was very aware of the stimulator and each time it went off I either lost my voice or coughed, but those side effects were short-lived. I was so excited; it was actually a comfort to know it was working. I continued with my psychiatric session and my psychiatrist laughed because every time the stimulator, I called it my "pacemaker for the brain," went off, I would cough. She laughed and said, "Three more coughs and your time is up."

I could feel my "pacemaker for the brain" working, but with each day the side effects became less noticeable. I began making plans for various activities, and I ended up with an out-of-state wedding in May and three conferences to attend in June. My girlfriend had determined that instead of driving, we would take a Greyhound bus to the wedding. Well, having never ridden on a Greyhound bus before it would be a new experience and I was actually ready to take the plunge and get out of my house for a week. Life was getting exciting. I was beginning to feel as if my depression was in remission.

In the meantime, I received a bill from the hospital for my surgery. Even though the bill was sent in error, it shocked me. The surgery had cost more than $46,800 which included the VNS device. Even though the figure seems high, it is a small price to pay for remission. It reminded me about what the Bible says about tithing in 2 Corinthians, "Remember this: Whoever sows sparingly will also reap sparingly, and whoever sows generously will also reap generously. Each man should give what he has decided in his heart to give, not reluctantly or under compulsion, for God loves a cheerful giver" (2 Corinthians 9:6–7, TAB). I had always been a cheerful giver and tithed regularly. God had performed a miracle in my life and given me back one hundred fold! Our God is so awesome!

Two weeks went by quickly, and it was now time for step three when my stimulator would be ramped up to .75 milliamps. I was a little apprehensive, but ready for anything at this point. Once again, my psychiatrist had me hold the wand over the implant and she turned it up to the next setting. Wow! Did I feel it this time? It felt as if there was a golf ball inside the left side of my neck. However, with each passing day, the golf ball got smaller and smaller until the feeling finally disappeared. There were times I felt the device go off and there were times when I never realized it. Overall, I remained comfortable with the increase.

Another two weeks passed by and it was now time for step four when my stimulator would be ramped up to one milliamp. There was no apprehension this time around. I was eager to see what would happen. The Cyberonic's © representative couldn't be there so my psychiatrist handled it herself. This time it felt as if someone had zapped me with a taser gun. I coughed repeatedly and struggled to catch my breath. Something told me this wasn't going to be easy to get used to and I was right. The first day I continued to cough, it remained uncomfortable, and I lost my voice completely when the device went off. The second day I stopped coughing, but it remained uncomfortable and my voice would fade out. The third day, it was a little less uncomfortable, but I would still lose my voice.

Please don't let this scare you away from VNS Therapy. Everyone is different and I was easily able to tolerate the uncomfortable feeling. There was no pain involved. It was a situation of "mind over matter," and most of the time I was too busy to realize the stimulator was activating. Each day improved and soon I didn't feel it anymore.

The wedding was beautiful, and the seminars were extremely educational. I had a great time. There was nothing to worry about except for the fact that I was still suffering from short bouts of depression along the way and I still didn't have a job.

The literature had stated that it may take six months to a year to notice results from the VNS Therapy so I wasn't concerned. I knew it would work because God gave me the opportunity to have the procedure done.

I had a number of psychiatric appointments and attended a Peer-to-Peer group therapy session which seemed to help immensely. I was disappointed when it ended because I had made some wonderful new friends. I vowed to take the next one unless I was working and the hours conflicted.

I had to find a job with insurance benefits and the

anxiety was mounting. I was working with the Bureau of Vocational Rehabilitation and Goodwill Industries to find a job, but once again, the resumes kept going out and no calls came in. This was putting a strain on me emotionally and I grumbled to my psychiatrist that I was back in the closet again. She decided that at my next appointment she would ramp up the milliamps on my stimulator to 1.25.

I was now in transition. I was still desperately trying to find a job, work for my sister-in-law, and finish this book. Sounds great, but all I wanted to do was sleep. It was a relief not to have to go to work every morning, and the more time that passed, the easier it became to stay home. I didn't want to have to work and face the cold, cruel world outside of my protective walls. I was anxiety ridden to even go to the grocery store. I didn't want to see people, I wanted to be invisible. The anti-psychotic drug Zyprexa that I had been on months earlier caused me to gain sixty pounds. Once I went off it, I quickly lost ten pounds, but still had at least forty pounds to go. My clothes didn't fit so I mostly lived in sweat pants. I was too tired to take care of myself. I would manage a shower almost every morning, but beyond that, my hair was as listless as I was and make-up took too much effort to apply. I let myself go. The extra weight, the smoking, and careless dress became ordinary. What happened to that young professional woman who wore dark blue suits, patent-leather heels, had groomed hair and nails, and applied just the right amount of delicate make-up to give a polished look? I was slowly unraveling—all the more reason to stay sequestered in my house.

Job prospects were slim to none. Once again, I began sending out resumes one after another. After thirty resumes and no interviews, my job representative helped me tweak my resume. She told me to send out twice as many resumes every week. I wondered, *to whom*? *Would I ever get back to work again and stay for more than one day?* I had to fight my insecurities and trust in God to lead me to the right job. I couldn't help but wonder, *what did God have planned for the rest of my life?* I hated what depression did to me. It took my mind, my strength, my hope, and my job. It took all of me and left nothing but a shell.

Finally, I received two calls in one day for interviews. My heart raced as I put extra copies of my resumes in my portfolio. Maybe I could do this after all! The interviews went well, and I patiently waited for a phone call telling me I had a job. But, once again, time came to a stand still and the hours and days dragged on. Lord, I prayed, *your will be done, not mine. If you want me to have a certain job then show me, give me a sign. I will graciously do your will.* Shortly thereafter I had a third call for an interview and I started feeling much better. Maybe there was hope of getting back to full-time work.

The first job I had hoped for didn't come to pass. They called to say they had filled the position. Then a second call came stating they had filled the second position. This left one more opportunity and more resumes to send out.

But, I trusted in God to lead me to the right position. He had graciously brought me this far, and I knew he wouldn't forsake me. God does not guarantee us a life that is safe and free from difficulty. We cannot predict what will happen to us today or tomorrow, but, as Christians, we can find rest in knowing that God has promised to never leave or forsake us.

In the meantime, I received a call from my sister-in-law informing me she was "letting me go," because I was making too many mistakes. It hurt me, but at the same time I immediately felt a strong sense of peace. God was preparing my circumstances to bless me with a greater opportunity. I prayed to God for his help and doubled my efforts to find a full-time job with benefits.

On June 28, 2007, I had my Vagus nerve stimulator ramped up to 1.25 milliamps.

The sensation was extraordinarily unpleasant. At this point, I thought maybe I had overdone it and my psychiatrist would have to take it back down to 1 milliamp, but I toughed it out. The unpleasant feeling lasted for a few days before it finally lifted. It's amazing how quickly I was getting use to it. Now I didn't have to see my psychiatrist for another month.

The best news was yet to come. I had been working with the Bureau of Vocational Rehabilitation but didn't have any luck so far. A friend of mine informed me about a job that had opened up at a Senior Housing Development where she lived. I immediately dropped off my resume with a well-written cover letter. They called me and scheduled an interview for the next day. When I went in for the interview, the job that I had applied for had already been filled. I was heartbroken, but the manager asked if I would be interested in a different position. It sounded interesting and she had me follow her to another building where the job was located. The more we talked, the greater the possibility of being hired became. Once again, God's timing is never late–I was offered the job on the spot!

This was a full-time job with benefits and a beautiful environment in which to work. Who could ask for more? God had blessed me with yet another miracle!

Good things come to those who love the Lord and to those who wait for his timing. His timing is always perfect. We have such an awesome God!

Things have changed. When my father and I see each other or talk on the phone, we always end the conversation with "I love you." My son and I have a wonderful relationship and he is planning to get married in 2008.

I don't know how things will work out from this point in my life, but I have managed to stay on the job and I'm delighted to be working again. It has now been several months and my depression has not returned. I'm once again beginning to feel human.

I spoke too soon. The job quickly became too much to handle with the combination of all the pills I was taking and the complicated job activities. My depression returned, and I felt like I was back at square one. I ended up having to quit my job because I wasn't able to do it and went back into my closet to wait it out. At this point I thought it best to try for Social Security Disability again.

I was getting help from the Bureau of Vocational Rehabilitation (BVR) and I finally got up my nerve to go back and tell them I quit because I couldn't do the work. I felt like a failure because in the past it would have been an easy job. But this wasn't the past and I was dealing with more baggage now that I had to pick up and carry along. When I went into the BVR office, Gidget, my job developer, smiled and giggled and waved her hand to say don't worry about it we'll find something else for you. After much discussion, it was decided that I would have to lower my standards to find a job that I would be able to do while on my medications that caused disorganized thinking.

We tweaked my resume again, and afterwards I thought, *I'm basically looking for a part-time receptionist job.* At first I was startled, but once I got home and had time to think it over, I realized a receptionist job wasn't bad. There were many responsibilities, and sometimes they even came with benefits. My hopes soared. If I could find something within a reasonable driving distance it would be worth it.

After a couple of months, things weren't working out, so I went back to my seasonal job at the department store. It was part-time, twenty to twenty-five hours a week in the stockroom, helping to unload trucks. However, it was something I could do, I liked it and loved unpacking the new clothes and not having to deal that much with the public, and my boss was wonderful. I told Gidget at BVR about the job and she said it wasn't on any of my sheets to find that type of job so they would have to begin a ninety-day follow-up period. That meant I had to meet with her two days a month to let her know how things were going and if she could help me with any problems. I said I could do that and the wheels were put into motion.

Before long, things were going smoothly so I got involved with the National Alliance on Mental Illness (NAMI). They had some wonderful peer-support groups that I attended and I thought they were so helpful that I decided to become a leader if possible. They needed leaders from my town, and I traveled to Columbus, Ohio to get three days of intensive training. Along with another facilitator, I now facilitate a NAMI Connection Recovery Support Group in our town. We meet once a week so it gets me out of the house and I like it. It's a peer-based, mutual support group for people facing the challenges of recovering from mental illness. Everyone has something to contribute and learn. We are a support group that focuses on allowing participants to share their experiences and learn from each other in a safe environment.

I was told I'd probably have more small bouts of depression and mania, but I believe they will be manageable. The VNS Therapy is working, although I recently had it increased to 1.50 milliamps. The biggest difference I've noticed is that I no longer have thoughts about suicide. If I continue to improve, I hope to get off some of my medication in the distant future. Even though there is no "cure" for my disease, there is peaceful remission for which I am extremely grateful. It's been a tough road, *but the sun is shining now and a beautiful rainbow appears on the horizon.*

There is always hope if you have faith in God!

My Spiritual Growth

"The thief comes only in order to steal and kill and destroy. I came that they may have and enjoy life, and have it in abundance (to the full, till it overflows)," (John 10:10, TAB*).*

I've come a long way in my 36 years of suffering from severe depression. I always believed in God, but never had a personal relationship with him until now.

My spiritual growth over the past eight years has played a dynamic role in my remission. I realize now that it is impossible to be perfect, and that's okay. I learned that as long as I believe in God and accept him as my personal Savior, I can repent of my sins and be forgiven. That means that each and every day I can start with a clean slate. All of my past transgressions have been forgiven and best of all forgotten. I accept myself for who I am. I don't want to be like everyone else anymore. I'm free to be me.

The masks are gone. God designed me in my mother's womb to be unique.

From my teenage years into my late forties I was insecure, lacked self-confidence and never spoke up for myself. My depression fed off my insecurities and my insecurities fed off my depression. But I know now that God has a plan for my life.

As Beth Moore states in her study of Daniel, God can deliver us from the fire and build our faith. He can deliver us through the fire and refine our faith, or He can deliver us by the fire and straight into His arms and perfect our faith.[1] God chose to bring me through the fire in order to refine my faith in him. He has a plan for my life that I'm not yet aware of, but it will be good because it is from God.

Jeremiah 29:11 NIV says, "For I know the plans I have for you," declares the Lord, "plans to prosper you and not to harm you, plans to give you hope and a future."

After all the trials and tribulations, depression, bipolar ups and downs, bad decisions, and messes I've made of my life, God still loves me and wants the best for me. His love endures forever and He will never leave me nor forsake me. He loves me unconditionally!

Joyce Meyer says, "We have to let God take us through things and let Him work in us so our mess becomes our message. Difficult things that we have endured in our past prepare us for God's blessings in our future."[2] My mess has now become my message to you!

Writing this book was difficult for me because I had to

relive the memories and feel the emotions of the bitter past. The heartache it caused was painful, but the experience was therapeutic because I see how far I've come. Please hear me when I say God can help you. He can help by bringing about a miracle in your life; He can heal you through a miracle, through the right medications, through proper therapy or through surgery. Meditate on the Word of God, study Scripture, memorize your favorite verses and watch yourself grow and change. Pray daily and give thanks to God for all the good things he has brought into your life. Praise God, worship God and know that God is God.

I want to express to you that throughout my life, even when I didn't know it, God was always there for me. He was picking up my precious pieces and working to get me on the straight and narrow path. God never failed me! I failed myself. As the Bible says in Proverbs 3:5–6 (NIV), "Trust in the Lord with all your heart and lean not on your own understanding; in all your ways acknowledge him, and he will make your paths straight." He is my strength, my mentor, my life! His son, Jesus Christ, died on the cross for my sins; his blood covered my sins and I have been forgiven. Isn't it fantastic that we have such a gracious and glorious God!

Our heavenly Father helps the needy and the poor. Humble yourself before God so that he can work in you to bring the miracle that he has brought into my life.

Keep on praying and trusting God, In Jesus' name I pray for all of you, Amen.

Appendix

Facts about Mental Illness

- Mental illness touches most everyone's life–either from personal experience or by knowing someone with a mental illness.
- During the course of one year, at least 20% of individuals will have symptoms of a diagnosable mental disorder.
- Mental illness occurs regardless of age, gender, race, ethnicity, culture, education, economic status, or place of residence.
- In 1997, the United States spent almost $71 billion on treating mental illness. The loss of productivity caused by the symptoms of mental illness resulted in an additional cost of $63 billion.
- Mental illness ranks first among all illnesses that

cause disability in the United States, Canada, and Western Europe.

- Of the leading causes of violent deaths worldwide–49% result from suicides compared with 31% for homicides and 19% for war.
- It is estimated that 1 of every 2 individuals with mental illness never receives treatment.
- Mental illness often affects other illnesses such as heart disease. Studies indicate that depression increases the likelihood of death following a heart attack.
- Mental illness has a biological and neurochemical basis. It is not the result of a character flaw or defect.3

"Major depression is a serious medical illness affecting 15 million American adults, or approximately 5 to 8 percent of the adult population in a given year" according to the National Alliance on Mental Illness (NAMI). "Among all medical illnesses, major depression is the leading cause of disability in the United States and many other developed countries."4

There is no single cause of major depression. Psychological, biological and environmental factors may all contribute to its development. Whatever the specific causes of depression, scientific research has firmly established that major depression is a biological medical illness.5

Depression isn't something you can just "snap out of" or "pull yourself up by your bootstraps." It is not a character flaw. Severe depression is usually caused by an imbalance of chemicals in the brain. It is a serious, often life-threatening, medical condition that needs to be treated.

Some Signs and Symptoms of Depression (That last two or more weeks)

- Insomnia or sleeping more than normal
- Feeling sad; depressed mood
- Loss of interest in activities or hobbies
- Low energy, feeling tired, fatigue
- Increase or decrease in weight
- Trouble making decisions or concentrating and slowed thinking
- Feelings of guilt, worthlessness, hopelessness and emptiness
- Decreased sexual activity

Suicide Signals

- Verbal clues, such as "You'd be better off without me"
- Expressions of hopelessness or helplessness
- Obsession with death
- Significant personality changes, including depression, moodiness or aggression
- Solitude to an excessive degree (not wanting to be around people)
- Sudden need to get everything in order

Take any of these signals seriously. Help the person seek immediate attention from a doctor, therapist, psychiatrist or clergy member. If you believe the situation is an emergency, call 911 immediately and do not leave the person alone.

Contrary to popular myth, those who talk about suicide are the most likely to kill themselves. Those who attempt suicide; tend to attempt again; in fact, the best predictor of an actual suicide is a previous attempt.

Another myth is that suicidal people have to "look" suicidal; they let themselves go, stop wearing nice clothes, stop wearing make-up, stop combing their hair and generally don't care about their appearance. In my case the opposite was true; I wanted to look my best when I planned my suicides!

Suicide Statistics

In 2004 the national death rate from suicides was 32,439 people. An average of one person every 16.2 minutes kills themselves. These statistics rate suicide 11th as a cause of death with homicide ranking 15th.

There were an estimated 810,975 annual suicide attempts in the United States in 2004 which translates to one suicide attempt every 39 seconds. This equates to 25 attempts for every death by suicide for the nation.

Suicide methods rank in the following order: Firearm suicides 51.6%; suffocation/hanging 22.6%; poisoning 17.9%; cut/pierce 1.8%; and drowning 1.1%.

Based on the 754,570 suicides from 1980 through 2004, it is estimated the number of survivors of suicides in the United States is 4.5 million (1 of every 65 Americans in 2004).6

Bipolar Disorder

Bipolar disorder or manic-depression is a medical illness that causes extreme shifts in mood, energy and functioning. These changes may be subtle or dramatic and typically vary greatly over the course of a person's life as well as among individuals. More than 3 million people in America suffer from bipolar disorder and the illness affects men and women equally.[7] Bipolar disorder is a chronic and generally lifelong condition with recurring episodes of mania and depression that can last from days to months. Although there is no cure for bipolar disorder, it is a treatable and manageable illness.

Some Signs and Symptoms of Mania

- Elated, happy mood, or an irritable, angry, aggressive mood
- Increased activity and high energy level
- More thought and faster thinking than normal
- Increased talking and rapid speech
- Grandiose plans
- Poor judgment
- Spending sprees
- Impulsive sexual indiscretion
- Decreased need for sleep
- Alcohol and drug abuse

Some of the medications I have taken over the past thirty-six years:

- Abilify (mania)
- Ambien (sleep aid)
- Ativan (anxiety)
- Buspar (anxiety)
- Celexa (depression)
- Cymbalta (depression)
- Depakote (mania)
- Effexor (depression)
- Elavil (depression)
- Geodon (mania)
- Haldol (schizophrenia)
- Klonopin (panic attacks and anxiety)
- Lamictal (anti-convulsant)
- Lexapro (depression)
- Librium (anxiety)
- Lithium (mood stabilizer)
- Muscle relaxers
- Pamelor (depression)
- Paxil (depression and panic attacks)
- Prozac (depression)
- Remeron (depression)
- Risperdal (antipsychotic)
- Serzone (depression)
- Sinequan (depression)
- Thorazine (antipsychotic)
- Tofranil (depression)
- Trazodone/Desyrel (depression)
- Wellbrutrin (depression)
- Xanax (anxiety)

- Zoloft (depression)
- Zyprexa (antipsychotic)

For More Information

NAMI (National Alliance for the Mentally Ill)
www.nami.org
888–999–6264

MHA (Mental Health America)
Formerly National Mental Health Association
www.mentalhealthamerica.net
800–969–6642

DBSA (Depression and Bipolar Support Alliance)
www.DBSAlliance.org
800–826–3632

CABF (Child & Adolescent Bipolar Foundation)
www.bpkids.org
847–256–8525

Cyberonics ©
100 Cyberonics Boulevard
Houston, TX 77058
www.VNSTherapy.com
877–669–4867

Endnotes

1. Beth Moore, *Study of Daniel*, (Nashville, Tennessee: Life Way Press, 2006), p 46.
2. Joyce Meyer, *New Day New You*, (Southlake, Texas: Improv. Ltd., 2006), p 37.
3. Building Better Tomorrows, Mental Health Association of Summit County, Inc., p 2.
4. Major Depression, National Alliance on Mental Illness, http://www.nami.org, p 1.
5. Ibid, p 1.
6. CDC WISQARS website "Fatal Injury Reports" and "Leading Cause of Deaths Reports," Suicide Date 2004, prepared for AAS by John L. McIntosh, Ph.D., December 15, 2006.
7. Understanding Bipolar Disorder, National Alliance on Mental Illness, Arlington, VA 22201–3042, p 1.